Edmond Jabès,
The Poetry of the Nomad

PETER LANG
New York • Washington, D.C./Baltimore • Boston
Bern • Frankfurt am Main • Berlin • Vienna • Paris

William Kluback

Edmond Jabès,
The Poetry of the Nomad

PETER LANG
New York • Washington, D.C./Baltimore • Boston
Bern • Frankfurt am Main • Berlin • Vienna • Paris

Library of Congress Cataloging-in-Publication Data

Kluback, William.
Edmond Jabès, the poetry of the nomad / William Kluback.
p. cm.
Includes bibliographical references.
1. Jabès, Edmond—Criticism and interpretation. I. Title.
PQ2619.A112Z73 848′.91407—dc21 97-41959
ISBN 0-8204-3833-2

Die Deutsche Bibliothek-CIP-Einheitsaufnahme

Kluback, William:
Edmond Jabès, the poetry of the nomad / William Kluback.
–New York; Washington, D.C./Baltimore; Boston; Bern;
Frankfurt am Main; Berlin; Vienna; Paris: Lang.
ISBN 0-8204-3833-2

Cover design by Andy Ruggirello.

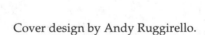

The paper in this book meets the guidelines for permanence and durability
of the Committee on Production Guidelines for Book Longevity
of the Council of Library Resources.

© 1998 Peter Lang Publishing, Inc., New York

Printed in the United States of America.

CONTENTS

Preface

Jabès refused to have followers. He turned to those who sought to be his companions and asked them to turn away, to follow their own feelings. Each man's existence embraces the nomadic journey. Each man is in the desert. Each man feels the indecision, the melancholic loneliness which plagues his soul. In each man, there is a conversation and a book. Man walks alone. He looks ahead and sees nothing. He looks backward and sees nothing. He looks above and finds emptiness. Man is before the divine. He searches for a refuge. He needs to escape. He cries to his God and asks why he has been left alone. Why are his cries silenced in the heavens? There is, and there will be, no help. Man will look about him and plead with his fellowman for understanding, but no man will understand. Each will turn to himself, to an ideology, to an orthodoxy, to a fanatic leader. Man flees the center. He looks for refuge. There is none. There are only fellowmen with a similar despair and restlessness, pain and disarray. A chaos hovers over man. Man cannot return to the desert. He can't leave it. He cannot put aside the book or the word. They are his creators. They are the essence of his experience. His reason is his only consolation. It grows weaker and weaker. A madness approaches him. What can stop it from coming upon him? How does he hold it back? An elusive hope has often betrayed him, tortured him, and driven him into the wilderness, into chaos. Man prays. There is nothing else to do. Prayer, he believes, is efficacious. In the end, it is prayer alone which is man's anchor. Prayer is man's poetry. The poet in him is his redeemer. Jabès sings the prayers of the poet. In prayer, there is consolation.

My book is a meditation on a journey which has never ended. I imagined my conversations with Jabès. I imagined his presence. I listened to him. I have not gone my own way. Jabès knows that my way will always belong to him. In our endeavors, in our loneliness, we are dependent upon each other, as others are dependent upon us. This is a book for every man. Each of us must discover his or her soul. This is a command of life. There are no escapes. I ask the reader to follow the poet. I ask him to remember those inimitable lines of Homer with which he begins the *Odyssey*:

> Sing to me of the man, Muse, the man of twists and turns driven time and again off course, once he had plundered the hallowed heights of Troy.[1]

I ask the reader to remember the journey of Israel and the man Moses. Remember much, oh man, before you begin your wanderings.

---

[1]Homer: *The Odyssey*, Translated by Robert Fagles, Penguin Books, 1996.

Introduction

Reading, like writing, is an experience. The experience can be neither limited nor controlled; it develops a logic, a life of its own. Reading Edmond Jabès was, at first, a curious and uncertain adventure. Exiled in 1956 from Egypt, he settled in Paris. Jabès wrote books with enticing titles: *The Book of Questions* (seven volumes), *The Book of Dialogue, The Book of Resemblances, The Book of Shares*. These titles were their initial attraction. They caused me to open the books. With a book in hand, I glanced at the first pages. I saw the wondrous closeness of prose and verse, of invented rabbis and their dialogues. My reading had begun in earnest. Curiosity yielded to mystery and mystery to persistence. Page drew forth page, and the adventure commenced. Jabès was writing the odyssey of Israel. The ancient adventure was alive, and deeply meaningful. It embraced the survival of an ancient tribe which had been devoted to a book, had experienced the desert of wonder, the frightfully powerful history of unending exile. Long ago, it was told that this people would dwell alone, but prophecies are heard and forgotten. Now we have these seven volumes of *The Book of Questions*. We ask, why are there only seven and not seventy, or seven hundred? The questions will never end, their truths shatter answers. The people bearing these questions have assumed a fate which lives in images and metaphors, parables and paradoxes.

Jabès, driven from Cairo to Paris, from the desert to the book, from the ancient land of Israel's exile, dwelt until his death in 1991 in the city of French culture, amid poetry, literature and the arts, which had always dignified this capital. He would write, contemplate his exile, the desert, the book. Here he would ponder the destiny of a people caught in a history in which the realities of exile became actualities. This people would reveal to the world what it meant to bear these realities and be dispersed, tortured, and tormented. Jabès's work is not an odyssey of woe. It is a longing to inquire, to discourse, to converse. Answers fade into questions as questions become answers. The reader is fascinated by this poetry of discourse, by the unquenchable searches and wonders of rabbis and their dialogues. We learn to wander with Jabès from place to situation, from verse to prose, and from prose to verse. We seem never to be satisfied. We are driven to further adventures.

The poet is tireless in his inquiries. We no longer allow answers to hinder our wandering, to limit our images and metaphors. If we tire, it is only for the moment. We regain composure, and we go on. What began as curiosity became an insatiable longing to travel the journey of an exiled people.

This is a book of meditations on the poetry of Jabès. What began as a single chapter became the beginnings of a book which will have no end, no island of rest. A book is always the source of books, as images bring forth images. Little do we control what we write or the dimensions of our reading. Nevertheless, we must be prepared for what we read and write. Experiences hover over experiences. They confront each other and do violence to each other. There is an excitement in writing about a poet who has become a partner in dialogue, who leaves you restless and desirous. Excitement becomes enthusiasm. We are forced to leave settled habits and positions, to investigate new possibilities, to see new visions, and dream the dreams of life.

Rabbis, exiles, the book, concentration camps are signs that point to the Jewish reality, and the writers who use them are most often Jewish writers. Jabès is a believer in the Jewish experience. He is not a voice of orthodoxy, a traditional believer. He is not a man of answers. He is a questioner in whom Jewishness is always becoming, but never *is*. He inquires and searches. He is the poet of the book of exile. He has gathered about him what he knows to be the most precious tradition of Israel: the constancy of discussion. This discussion, which emphasizes man's relationship to God, to the neighbor, and to the world, is Israel's legacy, the fate of a tribe which has never ceased to hold tenaciously to its book and its rabbinical discussions. Israel is *a* teacher of humankind. It makes no pretentions to divine privilege. It lives with its loyalties, loves, and persistence; it refuses to surrender them to either Christianity of Islam. Israel needs to dwell alone spiritually. The book is a revelation of the amazing experience of Israel. It can only be told by a poet who knows the desert, who creates images, and knows paradoxes.

In a series of dialogues with Jabès, Marcel Cohen asked him about a statement made by the Jewish philosopher Emmanuel Levinas, who said: "To ask myself questions about Jewish identity means one has already lost it, but one still clings to it, otherwise one would avoid the interrogation." Jabès replied: "I believe that we create our identity through that interrogation. To be Jewish would therefore mean to become it, step by step. At each step we would only be on the point of becoming Jewish. This would also mean that we couldn't be Jewish constantly. The affirmation 'I am Jewish' is already a regression, a stop, a way of falling asleep in that condition."[1] In this commentary on Emmanuel Levinas, Jabès directed his readers to that intimate dialogue between doubt and faith which accompanies his ventures into Israel's destiny. Without it there would be no adventure.

Jabès is the poet who began a curiosity and became an inseparable companion. I believe that the sensitive reader can imagine why it is not easy to travel with Jabès. Each of us has called himself into question, has doubted the sacred traditions, the tales of faith, and the authoritative voice. We struggle to feel the powers which drew Jabès to the varied images which emerge from the imagination, from the spiritual voyages of a soul which has no rest.

Nothing exists for us which does not find in questioning an ongoing discourse. Questioning is never arbitrary. It is the character of the inquiring soul to expand and embrace. Our mortality is in the questions. Where this is threatened, our humanity is endangered. Tenacious loyalty to Israel belongs to the need for discourse. Israel is distinct from its neighbors. Its reality is always coming into existence. Its God is presence in absence. Its book sends forth books. Its dreams have only dreams to preserve them. Jabès's Jewishness was poetical. It lived in his poetry. It was in his images, metaphors, and dreams. He was its fate.

We dwell with Jabès in commentaries and dialogues. He is our guide in the ventures of the spirit. His death in 1991 took him physically from us, but it has left us his soul. At the moment the material quality of the book fades away, Jabès speaks to us as presence in the present. For those of us who are receptive to adventures, who prefer the unknown to the known, the unexpected to the expected, the possible and contingent to the necessary and the determined, Jabès is the beloved companion. Thinking men are perplexed. The poet is our friend in perplexity. He shares with us his images and paradoxes in order that we, like him, may become commentators and creators of images and paradoxes.

The book was written to reveal the way into the desert of formless forms and soundless sounds. Jabès showed me a direction. I followed it from the known to the unknown. I have learned to live in the unknown, to dwell with uncertainty, to grasp the odyssey which carries life from necessity to contingency, but never from contingency to necessity. The poet shows us a way. His direction is the beginning of discourse. It is the way of wonder.

---

[1]*From the Desert to the Book: Dialogues with Marcel Cohen* (Barrytown: Station Hill Press, 1990), 67.

1

In the Sands of the Desert

With hesitant words, I enter the realm of a poet whom I have never personally known, but whose works lie before me and upon my shelves. How do I proceed, startled by the defiant whiteness of my paper, the eagerness of my mind to speak, my pen to put down words? I have read much, but I suspect the meaning of what I have read. The written word does not tell me its truths. Have I understood the words that were on the page? I never spoke of them to another. I merely assumed that they had meaning, and often I realized how faint was my understanding. But I want to converse with Edmond Jabès, to discover if there is a relationship between us, and if I can give this imagined relationship form and tone. What I am inclined to write about Jabès is not difficult to indicate, although I cannot explain why I move in this direction. His dialogues with the novelist and poet Marcel Cohen are called *From the Desert to the Book*. His conversations with his Judaic tradition begin with *The Book of Questions*.

How often I have felt captured by the moving forms of the desert, the powers that assemble in the book, the sacred Book. The book reveals and hides, communicates and baffles. It is the source of the unceasing questions and talks which refuse to leave the spirit. The questions come from our demons, the sources of life and movement, the feelings that are happily never fulfilled in answers. The answers are like wonders that enchant us for the moment, and then fade away. We are tossed by the fury of the questions and finally retire in quietude, exhausted by the storms which our questions foster, and the need to escape from them.

In exile from land and people, the poet found domicile in the exile of the spirit. Domicile in exile is the way of Jabès. There is no country for him. There is the realm of the spirit, the search for the book that came from the desert where forms fade into forms and where the quietude of the sands and the stars left openings for the divine revelation. In the desert, we meditate on the sands. Whether Jabès was in Cairo or Paris, his thought was in the desert, in the book that emerged and emerges from it. Not in the towns or in the cities is the message heard, but in the severe loneliness of the sands. Here the contrasts are distinct. Nature reveals her differences with painful contrasts. Man becomes accustomed to the moderations and compromises of urban life with its unending discussions and mental subtleties. The poet of the city has to live in two worlds. His visions and reveries remain with the desert, but he cultivates his words in the ambiance of urban life. Exiled from both the city and desert, the poet dwells in both. He is the poet of the exile. In the desert, his words are those of the city. In the city, he meditates on the sands of the desert. How do we walk between the two, become the juggler who must balance this life between contrasts, knowing that the book he searches for has already been revealed by the God of the desert and has been brought by his people to cities, to be studied and revealed in commentary? The book remains more than commentary. It is the primordial Book that comes to man in many forms, and refuses to be exclusively one or the other. The book will always be the possession of the desert, and only the acquisition of the city. Man knows that the book is of the landless lands, of the spirit that is always more than the spirit.

The Book of Questions begins with these words: "You are the one who writes and the one who is written."[1] At first we find such an idea bizarre. We are the masters of our thinking and our writing, but if we meditate upon the problem, we discover that what we write is conditioned by what must be written. We write only what we can write. We are an instrument of a spiritual demon that writes in and with us. We, the makers of ideas, are the consequence of a Maker who has written them upon us. We are not alone in the universe. We dwell with many spiritual realities which touch and come to live with us. The divine presence embraces all that we do and lives within all that is. This presence is in, and beyond Being. It is the source of Being, its creator and sustainer. We live in wonder of what is, and is yet to be. Our gaze is, as the philosopher said, upon the starry heaven above us and the spirit within us. We are men of dreams. We move from desert to city and from city to desert. We have no domicile. We are forever *on the way,* finding no land to call our own. A destiny greater than all fixed abodes carries us forward. We are men who not only speak, but who are spoken to, who hear not only the words and sounds about us, but those which come from other places and in other forms. Life for us is more than our surroundings, it is a universe

---

[1]*The Book of Questions* vol. I (Middletown: Wesleyan University Press, 1976), opening quotation.

of sounds and tones, of words and forms. It is the search for the book that was never written, but is always being written.

We turn again to Jabès's conversation or dialogues with Marcel Cohen. We listen to the questions and the answers, but in every good conversation there is the other who also listens and feels that he belongs. I assume that I belong to these conversations as I write commentaries to them and to myself. At the beginning of his dialogues, Jabès wrote: "Maybe *The Book of Questions* is the question made book. No answer – no matter how persuasive – will ever have enough strength to resist indefinitely the question that sooner or later will summon it. An idea so sure of itself that it would no longer take into account other ideas is dead before it is born. Today, more so than in the past, to accept nothing – even provisionally – that has not already somewhat resisted its systematic questioning, should be a basic principle. The question has always been, is, and will remain our best political weapon."[2]

The question is more than a political weapon. Its origin lies in the reality of the divine, at the source of the book. The question belongs to the book, as the question and the book precede all questions and all books. The book which is both the sacred and profane tale of mankind, was from the beginning with God. God is the ultimate Question which makes the book possible. The question is the constant and reemerging *why* that relates the book to the question, to the question which Moses put to God in the burning bush and from which he heard these words: "I am who I am," or, "I will be who I will be." In these words, nothing is said and everything revealed. The question is stated. We realize that without the question, there is no book, and the book is the question. We are the questions that are between the book and the question. We live to question. In and through the question we discover what it means to envision the book which is the cause of mankind's questioning. The book bears with it *The Book of Questions*, *The Book of Dialogue*, and *The Book of Resemblances*. We slowly discover a subtle dialectic between the book and the question, the dialogue and the resemblance. The latter two came forth from the revelation of the book. They are dependent upon the book.

They were already in the book. The book is the opening to worlds of creations, it spews realities that grow from it. They were already in it. We hear Reb Alcé say: "Mark the first page of the book with a red marker. For, in the beginning, the wound is invisible."[3]

To question is to enter the book. Every question is a search for an entrance. We don't know at first how to question. We put forth arbitrarily a question here and there and probe a way to enter the book.

---

[2]*From the Desert to the Book*, opening quotations.
[3]*The Book of Questions*, opening quotation.

"To take the wrong door," Jabès observed, "means indeed to go against the order that presided over the plan of the house, over the layout of the rooms, over the beauty and rationality of the whole. But what discoveries are made possible for the visitor! The new path permits him to see what no other than himself could have perceived from that angle. All the more so because I am not sure that one can enter a written work without having forced one's own way in first."[4]

Questions flood the book, each attempts to force its way upon the book, to find replies to that wondrous search for meaning that plagues the human soul. God, the universe, nature need questions. Without them both man and God would die. They abide for each other. History is the story of their questioning relationship. The questions are many but few allow us to approach "the beauty and rationality of the whole," the marvel that lies at the source of reality. The question requires preparation, and each man brings with him a way of questioning. Some are learned from the great human dialogues, others are found in the imagination, the awe before the sublime, and the enchantment that lies in the beautiful. Jabès found sublimity in the desert: "I would often stay for forty-eight hours all alone in the desert. I wouldn't take any books, only a blanket. A silence of that order makes you feel the nearness of death so deeply that it becomes difficult to bear any more of it."[5]

Jabès dreamed in the desert, but he also left us memories of his life in Cairo. Reality emerges from the contrasts and reconciliations we find in life, from the adaptations which we are forever forced to make. We struggle to weave these into patterns we call life, into perspectives from which we question the universe, and seek to comprehend its paradoxes. We want more than resolutions of parables, we know that these are meaningless. We need those questions which we rarely know how to ask, to find relationships between ourselves and the book. "In the desert," Jabès tells us, "one becomes other; one becomes the one who knows the weight of the sky and the thirst of the earth, the one who has learned to take account of his own solitude. Far from excluding us, the desert envelops us. We become the immensity of sand, just as we are the book when we write."[6]

The book came forth from the desert and settled in the cities; it grew in the experience of the vastness of the metaphors and analogies of the sand and the wanderings of the people; it came forth from the loneliness of desert revelations where tranquillity and sound reflected cosmic forces, where command and Word corresponded to the sharpness of

---

[4]*From the Desert to the Book*, 3.
[5]Ibid., 14.
[6]Ibid., 16.

contradictions. The Word appeared in harsher contrast to the eternal silence of nature.

Jabès remembered the Holy Days service at the great synagogue in Cairo. He remembered accompanying his father who always had a reserve seat, and he recalled the chants. Jabès spoke of the Jewish chant as the "infinite modulation of the word emerging from the holy words of the text." The chant was the conversation between man and God. The soul spreads its joys and pains, its supplications and longing before its Creator. "In the synagogue," Jabès notes, "it is the very words of the sacred, immutable text that let their chant be heard, allowing nothing other to be heard or seen than the word, the infinity of the letter."[7] The chant is the embodiment of the history of the people spoken to God in the wailing monologues of song. We are captivated by the melodies of suffering and faith, of defiance and submission. We listen as the words fill the synagogue. They flow in and out of the hearts of the faithful. The melodies are the questions that fill the book. They are the commentaries intoned to God. Man is aware of the divine presence, of that sacred rhythmic dialogue that is only possible in contrition and love. Through the ages, the melodies became poems, the poetry of prayer. The melodies came from Jubal, a descendant of Cain, a sufferer upon the earth, who had taught man that he is not his brother's keeper. We sing of our sins and our punishments, like children before a just and loving father. The questions come from hardships. The book is the sacred history of the sufferings of love.

Marcel Cohen posed the following question: "When you left Egypt (1956), you never considered, for a second, settling in Israel. And yet you feel deep concern for that country?"[8] The problem of a domicile exists only for those whose spiritual and physical dwelling are not the same. It does not arise for those who belong to a people with a fixed abode and language, but for those who live in conflicting worlds, who dwell in and among a people, but belong to the destiny of another. Jabès was French-speaking and could work only in a nation that could receive his works, and in which he could find listeners.

There is another world, the history of Israel, the land of Israel, the book of creation, the glories and the sufferings of a tribe who believed they were chosen by their God to be a message to humankind. Jabès described the conflicts that lived within him concerning the reality of belonging. He said: "Maybe there is something deeper still, something I constantly broach in my books, and that is my visceral repugnance to

---

[7]Ibid., 20.
[8]Ibid., 26.

being rooted anywhere. I feel that I exist outside of my belonging. That non-belonging is my very substance."[9]

There is non-belonging in all belonging that is other than physical existence. Every being who thinks and feels knows that he lives in more than one world. There are realms of reality we have not as yet begun to comprehend or touch. Jabès does not seek to submerge his Jewishness in the land of the French. He is subservient to no realm, to no doctrine and ordinance, and yet he is not a free spirit. He dwells in many lands and peoples, but in each he exists differently. He is a French poet and a son of Israel, a son of France and a poet of Israel. He is committed to that journey which takes him from the desert to the book. He journeys in lands of paradoxes and parables. Jabès wrote *The Book of Questions*; he could begin with no other reality. He believed that human existence began, and begins, in questions, that these are the "foothills" of dialogues. Are there really beginnings, or only beginnings of beginnings, since all beginnings are already in the book which is the book of beginnings.

"That non-belonging – with the availability it allows me – is also what brings me close to the very essence of Judaism and, generally, to the Jewish destiny. In a certain way, Judaism is but questions asked of History."[10] We feel perplexed thinking of Judaism as the questions asked of history. Judaism seems more wrapped in its ordinances than open to questions, but this is the fate of religions which become more and more hardened by the necessities of daily existence. Jabès draws us back to that realm of questions which plagued the thinkers and poets of great faiths, enticed to reveal wonders and bring us to that space where man and God approach the mysterious embrace. The word of God must always be the word of man, but are not the words of man the silence of God? Man seeks from God the meaning of human history and the destiny of the future. The silence of God brings him closer to his perplexities. How does he live in a world of divine silence? The Word becomes silence. Man questions it relentlessly. He calls his questions the rupture of his non-belonging. His worldly dwelling is his non-belonging. He dwells where his non-belonging is the source of his reality. He knows that the dialectical quality of life brings together the oppositions of belonging and non-belonging, but this coming together is not a fixed solution, it is the touchings of contrasts, approaching each other, attempting to speak with each other. Everything remains fluid and undetermined. We are helplessly left with only the *why*, the unknown and the silent. We are never freed from our wanderings, searching

---

9Ibid., 29.
10Ibid.

constantly for the book which will always be the book but never our book.

Jabès observed that "by asking himself 'Who am I', every Jew also puts forth the question of the ambient culture in the West. The two questions are inextricably linked. For the Jew, to question means always to keep open the question of the difference."[11] Israel constitutes the radical difference within both the Christian and Muslim faiths. The *whys* of the survival belong to the secret of the book. They live from its primordial revelations and have commented upon them through the ages. Israel has dwelt with its neighbors but has never become a part of them. These neighbors have always sought its birthright: to live from the question. Israel's presence questions the truths of the other faiths. Their longing for totality is rejected by Israel. Israel declares and maintains its faith in the book. Truth is sought only to hide the divine. In truth God becomes exclusive. Truth shatters divinity. Truth belongs to the quality of human affairs. In fear of God's holiness man seeks human truth about God. Israel symbolizes this opposition everywhere and always. Israel's message – which it reveals and hides – is the difference between truth and holiness.

Truth is the truth only of an object. Wisdom and holiness reduce man to awe of God. They force him to be humble and limited in his pretentions and desires. Where this distinction is held to be binding, the sacred separation between man and God is preserved with love and contriteness. Separations belong not only between God and man, but remain between man and nature, between man and man, and ultimately between dream and reality. Nothing agitates us more dogmatically than the search for truth in human affairs, i.e., in science, technology, in sociology and psychology, in all those activities in which we claim to control the dimensions of our work and the elements that are active in it. But nothing is more damaging and destructive to human affairs than the search for truth through history, literature, or poetry, in every realm of life where human domination must be limited by the powers of the divine spirit and light. They illumine the mind and make it possible for reason "to see" this dependence of love on transcendence.

Cohen put forth this statement for Jabès's comment: "Egypt appears in none of the poems from *Je bâtis ma demeure* [I Build My Dwelling] written in Cairo. But it becomes obsessive in *The Book of Questions*, the seven volumes of which were written in Paris." Jabès replied: "The writer, like the historian, lends meaning to the past but, contrary to the latter, he destroys the past by giving it form. The writer does not try to be the witness. He is only there listening to the words that trace his

---

[11]Ibid.

future."[12] Jabès had spoken of non-belonging as the substance of his life. He is a witness to the non-belonging, to a past that has meaning which prepares the road of his future. He selects from the past; he never seeks to reflect it. The poet creates the future from the past. He wants the past to speak to the generation to come, to illumine the road ahead. Humankind can bear witness only to a fragmentary past. We are always selecting and constructing, giving form and an architecture to what we have chosen. Israel lived in chosenness, hoping to see in it divine love and privilege, but chosenness is a way of building, of putting forth a message. Chosenness is a moral burden and ultimately a mystery and a wonder. We sing and chant its meaning; we write its messages in poetic reveries, but we remain in awe of its peculiar forms and reality. We know what we should not say and do. We know that mystery and dream are beyond truth. They move us toward the holiness of God. We listen to the words of the past not simply to hear them, but more significantly, to hear what they are not saying. We cannot hear revelation. We wait, in hope, for what is yet to be seen and heard.

There is no escape from the book, from the memories of it, from the longings for it and the sacred separation that always keeps the book at a distance from us. The book is always *there* but never *here* with us. "This is the Book of God through which God questions himself. And there is the book of man. It is on the scale of God's."[13] The book is old, it was in the beginnings. It belonged to the seas and the skies, to the air and the light. The book belongs to our remembrances; it is the book of remembrances; it is the book of life, inseparable from remembrances. We become men through memory, through the past which we bring forth in remembrances. The family of humankind is born in remembrances. We write from our memories; we create the bonds that link us not only to origins but to futures, to new forms and new hopes. The books which we write, those which help us seek out the forms of the past, of the divinity that brought forth our lives, reveal the constant movements of birth and death which mold the fragmentary quality of our existence. In this cycle of birth and rebirth the memories of humankind become the tissue of human life. We struggle to know what the cycle means to man, we want to know what the question means to him. We do not know what it means to God. How can we understand that God questions himself? We say it analogously. God can be the questioning one, allowing us to think about him as the questioning God, although we are the men who write *The Book of Questions*, who know that knowledge belongs to "an infinite unknowing," that truth belongs to the realm of falsity. God questions

---

[12]Ibid., 30.
[13]*The Book of Questions*, 20.

only the question for which he is the question. This is a parable which knows itself as a parable. Are not all the questions which man poses to God parables? Man speaks of God in parables. He speaks of reality in paradoxes.

The book has the shifting forms of the desert sands. The book abhors fixity and definition. It is the book because it never finds form but is always the book of questions. Man writes to discover forms. He wants to suppress the formlessness of the book. He wants to explore the absence of form. But is not the book the form of all forms, even the absence of forms? We think of the book as the realization of forms. We contemplate the realization of forms. We cannot live with the totality of forms.

Totality is madness, and madness is death. The world has given us witnesses of political and moral totalitarianism, and we have heard their tales and their memories of the madness that accompanies the demonic presence. We have prudently shunned those who have sought to impose visions of new orders and utopias. We have lived in fear of new divine revelations, new folk heroes who create new jargons in which doubts and contingencies lose their meaning.

Why are there so many talking rabbis throughout Jabès's works? They seem to be coming and going, adding a commentary or a question, and we wonder if these questions and commentaries could not be given by others. Jabès reminded us that the rabbis "are essentially the privileged interpreters of the book. For them, to find God means to find Him *in* the book, through the word that is hiding *behind* the word – as if there was always a book in the book and it was really a question of deciphering this book beyond the text, beyond the sign itself. A kind of white writing inside of writing."[14]

Every great book demands deciphering. It requires from the reader that it be rewritten. Every reader is a "rabbi" who, through the words he sees and comprehends, finds others that have not as yet come to his sight. Reading is imagining; it realizes the depths of subjectivity which in its essence is the deepest moment of objectivity. We are aware that the object is there for the subject, and becomes the realization of the highest subjective moment: the identification of subject and object. What other idea can we have but "the idea we have of ourselves"? In the imagination there is the movement from subject to object, there is the interplay of talking and listening. There is no separation, but the luminous interplay of hearing and being heard, of speaking and being spoken to. We speak of reading a book and we know that reading is possible only because we have read. The experience of the book is the ever presence of the history of humankind which here and there leaves

---

[14]*From the Desert to the Book*, 47.

traces of its reality in the varied parts of the world. We gather these traces and we write books of our dwelling, we write of our experience, of the journeys we have taken from the desert to the book. We relate a wandering and a wondering. The book becomes our commentary to the presence of the book which contains the full story of our journey in which God questions himself and we question the purpose of our existence. We learn to listen to our texts and find ways to bind them to our lives, for our lives were born from these texts. The texts tell us not only of the book which is in time, but of one that is beyond time, which hides and illumines what man searches to know. Jabès teaches us how to approach the varied levels of reality, to move from the known to the unknown and from darkness to illumination, knowing that these contrasts form the fabric of human existence. We become sensitive not only to what is given, but more importantly, to what has not yet been given, but awaits revelation.

"And Reb Hati: The pages of the book are doors. Words go through them, driven by their impatience to regroup, to reach the end of the work, to be again transparent. Ink fixes the memory of words to the paper. Light is in their absence, which you read."[15] Nothing dazzles us more than the interplay of whiteness and the writing of the words. The interplay reveals man's struggle for concreteness, the subtle and magic quality of the words which seek to avoid the definitions and the fixity which man needs for his physical abode. In the first page of the book which man writes to relate his wandering, there is "the wound," at first invisible, but more and more obvious as we read the tale of suffering which comes with the book. Man's most precious legacy from the generations, and his most valued gift to the future, is the book. He lives from and within the book which is a revealing reflection of the book, the eternal and encompassing holiness which is God. When man relates his history, he tells the story of the formation of the book. "All the secrets of the universe," Jabès stated, "are buds of fire soon to open, do I know in my exile, what has driven me back through tears and time, back to the wells of the desert where my ancestors had ventured? There is nothing at the threshold of the open page, it seems, but this wound of a race both of the book, whose order and disorder are roads of suffering. Nothing but this pain, whose past and whose permanence is also that of writing."[16] Everything remains to be revealed. We feel the presence of the beginning, awaiting that coming revelation. We know that the "buds" have yet to burst and God is yet to be revealed. We belong to the history of the Words, to a community that was formed to hear the Words as they

---

[15]*The Book of Questions*, 25.
[16]Ibid., 25-26.

sought to bind themselves to each other, to bring forth the variety of meanings which they can only imagine, imagine faintly.

"The Jew," Jabès reminded us, "is at the center of a vertiginous paradox: by inventing God he invented himself, so true is it that 'to choose is to be chosen,' God is the choice of the Jew and the Jew is the choice of God. The Jew has no choice except to remain true to that choice, if only because historical circumstances never gave him the possibility of really eluding it, of ceasing to be Jewish."[17] The question of God's existence is of little importance for a tradition which developed from the faith in its existence. The Jews decided to bear God into the world; they decided to be his children; they decided to suffer for his existence. Our lives depend upon the meaning of the tradition that bears within it this faith in God. Jabès spoke of "Judaism after God." This is the community that bears the consequence for God's presence in the world, which is determined to be the manifestation of his presence, and stubbornly refuses to surrender their faith to other religions. Judaism remains the faith of the question, the faith of a people who never cease to question their existence, their purpose.

The Jew is always moving toward truth which is beyond the horizon. "To go towards truth, that is the essential preoccupation of the Jew."[18] God has absented himself from the world and we must seek to discover what it means to bring back his presence. Our journey is one of rediscovery. Without God's absence, there would be no questioning, man would find no way to comprehend the freedom of the question. The rupture that is achieved through the divine silence provokes the question, the question of freedom. Man can search for truth only after God's abdication. Truth is elusive. Man has only the glimmers which fascinate and entice him. The Jew cleaves to his mission and its message. He bears witness to these glimmers of truth. He needs no proofs for his stubbornness and hope. He knows that his community is faithful to its mission. Its faithfulness is its truth.

"I only know," Jabès observed, "that due to circumstances, solitude has become the profound destiny of the Jew.... There is a moment when the words *opening, rupture, solitude* become one and the same word."[19] Israel is a people who dwell alone. Through the ages, we have heard the solitude. It speaks the destiny of the people. Solitude speaks of difference, but not of indifference. It speaks of the birthright that can never be alienated from the covenant that was not made among men, but

---

[17]*From the Desert to the Book*, 57-58.
[18]Ibid., 59.
[19]Ibid.

between the divine and Israel, a holy covenant that binds the human in the Word.

Rupture separated God from the creation, man from self-deification. The divine withdrawal gave the world to man, to the laws of necessity which man sought to understand, accept, and control. No longer could man induce the divine to return to a creation that now belongs to the sons of Cain, who are capable of work and thought, but who seek utopias and dreams that cannot be realized. They are limited creatures, tainted with evil. The human lot is a heavy one. Cain knew this well. But we live in spite of our woes and we struggle to live nobly. Again and again Jabès refers to the rupture, to that gap that lies between the book and the question. From the beginnings of human history, the question and the book have belonged to each other. There was never a question without the book, and the book was never without the question. Each question stirs the radiance of the book, each does it in its own particular and distinct way. In every question the book is born anew, in birth there is something unique. The great conversation through the ages has been between the book and the question. Jabès takes us on the precious journey through conversations between book and question, showing how deeply dependent they are upon each other, forcing us to realize that there is no book without a question and no question without a book.

Marcel Cohen asked Jabès if he agreed with the novelist and literary critic Maurice Blanchot that to be a Jew was first of all to be "the other," to assume the separation that he embodies in the presence of his fellowman. Jabès replied: "If the Jew is the other, it is because, trying at all costs to be himself, he is *also* each time a being from nowhere. That's where his difference and the distance at which he stands are inscribed."[20] I am struck by the phrase "a being from nowhere." Man needs to be from somewhere. From the moments of recorded history we read of man's search for a physical and spiritual domicile. Even if we believe that man is no more than a fragment or a nomad, we search for an order which moves each toward the other, revealing a rational force which drives things toward an order. What is "a being from nowhere" if not the being who never ceases to question, whose life becomes the question? He is the being who has a land, is identified with a people, and believes he can be like all other peoples, but knows that he cannot. He hears a message which the world never hears, which he knows can never be communicated. The divine message remains fragmentary. Each generation ploughs through its memories and reminiscences to find hints of the message. The message lives in dreams and poetic reveries and belongs to the universe, to the time before God withdrew from his world.

---

[20]Ibid., 60.

We live in the era of the rupture, in the world of the question. We question the world of appearances. What appears leaves us dissatisfied. There is a reality above and beyond the world we see. We search for its being.

The Jew is the stranger who knows how to live as the stranger, the one who dwells alone in the world, who no longer believes that he can find an answer in this world. He refuses to be a captive of an answer. This refusal to surrender in despair and hopelessness to the pessimism of a political and moral answer, to a philosophy of history that eliminates accident and contingency, is the sacred stubbornness of Jewish existence. This stubbornness which characterizes Jewish existence dwells with all who are strangers in this universe, who reject the quick solutions of the jargon makers, who know that their destiny belongs to the eternal *why*, to the book of questions, i.e., to the book of life. Our conversations with Jabès turn again and again to the journey of the stranger for whom every domicile is a path to another. There are no heroes among the strangers, there are only stubborn beings. They know that they can have no answers, that each step in life is a preparation for another, and each pitfall shows us the illusion of having found an answer.

Jabès said: "I believe that we created our identity through interrogation. To be Jewish would therefore mean to become it, step by step. At each step, we would only be just on the point of becoming Jewish. This would mean that we couldn't be Jewish constantly. The affirmation 'I am Jewish' is already a retrogression, a stop, a way of falling asleep in that condition."[21] Do we hope to find the answer to our identity, or do we know that the search for identity has no answer, but is only a further question, that this search continues in conviction and commitment? The answer would end the questioning, but we are questions, and with the answer we die. For centuries we have rejected the answers given by our sister faiths, by moral and political philosophies, who have not maintained the sacred quality of the question. With the question we have kept alive our freedom, the reality of exile and the experience of the stranger. In these spiritual realities, we created a language of rupture, of separation and estrangement. "Maybe exodus and exile," Jabès noted, "were indeed needed so that the word cut off from all words – and thus confronted with silence – can acquire its true dimension. A word in which nothing speaks any longer and which, to be totally liberated, becomes profoundly ours; just as we are truly ourselves only at the most arid core of our solitude."[22]

---

[21]Ibid., 67.
[22]Ibid., 68.

This is the word that liberates us from fixity and definition; it is the word that allows us to wonder and journey, it is the word that evokes the sands of the desert, that denies the fixed forms, that causes us to seek the subtlety of change and displacement. In every wanderer there is the desert, the source of forms and their disappearance. These words of the journey dwell in other words, but we realize that it is the word of the soul which creates and denies. This word negates the jargon of political and moral language; it is the word that questions the worlds of traditions in which the spirit hides and suffocates, and rises again to visions of new exiles and desert wanderings.

Abram wandered from the land of his father and "Abram journeyed by stages through the Negeb" (Gen. 12:9). This is the journey of exile which is made wherever the desert belongs to the spirit of the people, where there is a domicile beyond the domicile, a reality beyond realities, and a sacredness beyond truths.

2

In the Land of Silent Words

Our last remarks on Edmond Jabès led us to this statement: "Wandering creates the desert." The spirit must wander if it is to avoid the captivity of the fixed idea, if it is to escape both pessimism and optimism, if it is to journey freely from thought to thought, from image to image. Nothing brings the feeling of death more to poetic life than the captivity of the word. Images of the silently drifting sands, of the closeness of the heavens to the earth evoke the reveries and dreams in which the creative life finds its sources. We are born and reborn in dreams; we reveal in them the indomitable images of the spirit, the unquenchable need to give form and order to a fragmentary reality which escapes constantly. In this indomitable spirit lives the question which is more than a desire for a particular answer. It is the light in which we see reality. The question draws us away from the captivity of the answer. It tells us that the book is beyond our questions. The book is greater than our commentaries, and is at the same time the source of them. The harmony of paradise is no longer; there is only rupture. We struggle to keep the book with us, but it is not our possession – it belongs to the water, the earth, the fire. It stands over, but also beneath, us. It entices us and never yields to our longing. It remains hidden in the light it sheds upon us. We are children of the earth in search of the book. It is a loving father who knows that he must not become the possession of his child. The book belongs to us only in the question, in the realization that the book is, in truth, the book of questions.

Jabès remarked: "To question means to break; it means to set up an *inside* and an *outside*. It means to be at times in the one, at times in the other. Man *outside* that would be, in relation to the inside, a backing away, a recession – the retreat – the pre-prelude, the first threshold necessary for the interrogation; a neutral space where neutrality is absolute."[1] The question is indeed the break, the fact of the rupture. The question is and creates the power of inner life; it overcomes and is subject to the domination of the externality. The question subjects the *outside* to doubt and uncertainty, but is nevertheless dependent on it. The *outside* is incomplete. It is questioned from within. There is no autonomy or orthodoxy. The question puts man face to face with God. It forces him to shatter the external, to deny to it the right to shape and limit the consequence of the question. "After Moses," Jabès said, "the Jew claims for himself the privilege of a face-to-face relationship with God – no intermediary, not even Moses, stands between him and his Lord."[2]

Without intermediaries the Jew faced his God not only to worship his beauty, to be in awe of his majesty and holiness, but also to question him. He dared to question the creation, the purpose of the forms of life and the powers of his reason. Before God man does not whimper; he writes commentaries, he debates the ways of the divine; he clarifies the logic of the discussions and the unceasing desire to know how to speak of the divine ways. Man cannot let go of the divine; he struggles relentlessly to know God's ways. He formulates dialogues, and writes poetry to express his longings and desires for God. As long as he questions, he refuses to accept the finality of the answer, of a particular and unique revelation. The question takes him away from the deification of particular forms of religious practice. These are subordinate to his insatiable will to meditate upon the meaning of his dialogues with his fellowman about the divine. He does not search alone but in communion with others. He needs community and tradition. He cannot escape the realms of dialogues which his predecessors created, and in which he finds his own questions. These he pursues as if they were posed for the first time. He struggles to remain free of fixed forms and definitions, although these are needed by a believing community. He sees these limitations. He avoids giving them divinity.

Closeness to God means taking the Word seriously, to believe that it reveals God's will. The Word becomes the possession of the community, but it is always the Word *and* the commentary. The Word is never alone, otherwise it would overwhelm and destroy the one who hears it, or burn the lips of the one who speaks it. 'The relationship to God," Jabès stated, "can only be created through this word which will be questioned, then explicated – only to be questioned further, so as to convince oneself that it has indeed been heard, before one even considers how to answer it."[3] Where there is no Word there can be no question. Belief in the Word

---

[1]*From the Desert to the Book*, 71.
[2]Ibid.
[3]Ibid.

makes the question the substance of man. Man searches for himself through the question. He believes that there is a history and tradition of humankind, and that there is a purpose in history and tradition. We know that if we are persistent in our questioning, hints of the divine will be illumined, buds will open, and divine traces will be discovered. The divine has left us hidden sparks, enclosed shells, that can be opened through knowledge and goodness. There is no choice, but an optimism or pessimism which allows us to take the journey of the question. The message we carry in us is incomplete and in fragments. We know there is a message, but unlike the Fathers to whom it was given, we remain with a birthright whose pieces cannot be put together, and which yields to no singular interpretation.

In the divine absence we find the source of creation. The presence of God would destroy the question. Absence is the realization of what was or what can be. When we speak of the absence of God, we speak of creating a world in which the presence would reveal holiness and majesty. But in such a world there could be no human life. Human life begins in the divine absence, the source of creation. No reality is more significant for the understanding than the word *absence*, what is withdrawn, is no longer present, but is nevertheless the most significant reality. From our comprehension of absence, which is always incomplete and inadequate, we begin to grasp the importance of commentary and the preciousness of the Word. The Word is both present and absent. In its presence we die, in its elimination we are mad.

Marcel Cohen asked Jabès: "How did you discover the Talmud?" Jabès replied: "My father kept the eleven bound volumes of the Jerusalem Talmud in the Schwab translation on the desk. He had the books from his father and, like him, often immersed himself in them. I believe his Cartesian mind found reason for profound jubilation in the Talmud. I'm led to think that it was the implacable logic of rabbinical argumentation that seduced him, rather than the actual content. My father made me a present of these books – they are among the rare ones I was able to save – a few years before my departure from Egypt."[4] Jabès felt affection for these volumes and he studied them with surprising pleasure, finding in them a realm of argumentation that touched not only ethical and metaphysical speculations, but everyday existence with a rare and profound seriousness. No human action, relationship, is left undiscussed, no relationship between man and nature neglected. We wonder at the devotion of the rabbis to human life and we are deeply apprehensive of all faiths that denigrate the world, leaving us with a dualism, making it possible to give evil an ontological reality. The Jew

---

[4]Ibid., 72.

remains responsible for the goodness of the creation and for the Word that was spread upon it. He remains encompassed by the Word, replying to it ceaselessly with commentary. Its presence is his responsibility, and with love he cares for the divine sparks that are left to him.

"I feel," Jabès said, "that this represents an incredible difference from what will become Christianity. From it arises free choice, the audacity which gives the Jew the right to probe God in each vocable – thus also the appeal to his ability to understand, and a tolerance that accepts error as long as it is due to a sincere and authentic approach to the book."[5] What is refreshing about Jabès's observations is the idea of freedom inserted in the relationship between the Jew and the divine text. If this relationship embodies the tradition, then it is free to go beyond it, to interpret the text from changes in vision and perspectives. This freedom exists in all forms of human life. The Jew is alone with the text. He reads it to comprehend, to cite the authorities, but, above all, to create a reality between himself and the words. Each age hears the text differently. Each age must express the text differently. The text is not worshipped. It is studied and loved. The text makes possible both poetry and art. The text inspires. We are children of the text, but masters of books. Our freedom with the divine word makes it possible for us to be masters of the human word. We hear, and are passionate about, the Word. We have the confidence to write our texts. The listener becomes the master.

We always return to the nature of the question. Marcel Cohen remarked that "what is at stake is a vital, irreducible anxiety, a gaping breach subsisting forever between the question and the answer." To this, Jabès replied: "Does not the question wait for an answer only to be reborn from itself? It is the only vehicle of thought; it is, one could say, thought's trial all the way to the unthought that obsesses it."[6] The question is obsessed with an answer, with a passionate search for the book which cannot be the possession of man. The love with which man searches makes it possible for every question to surpass itself, to generate a new question. The book is, however, always presence. Presence is not present, presence is in absence!

In his opening remarks to the fifth book of *The Book of Questions, Elya*, Jabès stated: "In back of the book there is the ground of the book. In back of the ground there is immense space and, hidden in the immense space, the book we are going to write in its enigmatic sequence. Everything is before Everything. The word is the day after the word, and the book the day after the book. So we turn forever around what was and will be and which, in the image of God's proud absence, stays what is, namely: the

---

[5]Ibid., 73.
[6]Ibid., 75.

mysterious tie to the universe and the place where the universe waits to be discovered."[7] When we turn from the realities that are around us, when we decide not to be overwhelmed by them, then we realize there are others that touch deeply the sources of creative life. We become aware of the fact that the question does not simply open a dialogue but that it shatters the reality about us. "Questioning is, in itself, violence, because it provokes the violence of the answer and, in turn, inflicts violence on it."[8]

The violence of the question is alive in the violence of the answer. The question attempts to overturn a tradition, to shatter an answer, to give reign to a new answer. Questions undercut the dominance of commanding positions. They are the negations of what exists. The question lives in the answer, as the negation is always present in what dominates. Thought is carried through on the chariot of negation, or if we return to the word *absence,* we discover that absence is the question that lives in every reality. No matter what word we use, we struggle to grasp the same relationship: the violence we call negation comes forth in the question. The question is a truth which confronts another. We are not concerned with the conflict of truth and falsehood, but with confrontation of truth with truth. This is the dominant problem. It causes us distress. How do we relate truth to truth? Knowing that we are no longer in control of truth, that we live among fleeting truths, we either seek to replace one by another or we learn to live with a multiplicity of truths; we learn to be indifferent. In indifference we lose that singularity of devotion that tries to maintain the validity of the answer. Indifference is neither the question nor the answer; it hides from the violence that breaks forth from the question, that seeks to shatter the answer. Truth, in opposition to truth, can become tolerant, but tolerance deprives truth of its violence. Is there truth without violence? The question that seeks for truth needs to shatter its rival, it needs to proclaim the dignity of the answer, to destroy the nature of the previous answer and establish its supremacy. The journey of the spirit cannot avoid the violence which drives it from question to answer. The spirit brings violence. Violence is its life.

From where does the lie emerge? The lie is the idolatry of a truth, a demonic exaggeration of a form or an idea. The lie is embodied in the absolute value we confer upon a truth. If we accept the reality of the lie as the demonic exaggeration of a truth, then we affirm that every truth which seeks to attain exclusivity becomes idolatry. But can there be a

---

[7] *The Book of Questions, Yaël, Elya, Aely* vol. 5 (Middletown: Wesleyan University Press, 1983), 121.
[8] *From the Desert to the Book,* 75.

religious truth that remains relative, and yet sustains the confrontation of the question and its validity? If we agree that such a truth is possible, we are removed from the spiritual journey of man, from the dialogue of question and answer, from man's face-to-face relationship with the text, from the history of this relationship. If we deny such a truth, we return the spirit to that intimate and precious dialogue between question and answer to man's quest for the book. Whatever position we assume, we realize that the human condition, the trust in man's capacity to think and act, demands a comprehension of violence as the motor force of the journey in search of the divine.

Jabès noted that there is an order to the questions, and that in this order we discover the way man seeks the answer. But what is the answer man seeks? Does it imply a final answer or an answer that embodies a question? The answer is only the exhaustion of the question, the final answer; the total exhaustion of the question. The more man believes he approaches an answer, the more he is aware of the decline of his spiritual powers. The answer becomes the refuge, the harbor of the infirm and tired. The answer is the fortress which tries to ward off the question. The answer collapses before the question, and with it man feels the approach of death.

Jabès wrote that "the Jew has himself become question." The more we become knowledgeable of Jewish thought, the more we comprehend Jabès's remark. There is no doubt that every Jew feels an attachment to the cycle of the calendar, to the fundamental separations made between what is permitted and prohibited in daily life, but there is always a more or less. What is fundamental is that the Jew is free to speculate about God, the peoplehood of Israel, the Messiah, and the meaning of Israel for the world and the other faiths. The complexities of these speculations are so extensive that it is impossible to characterize Jewish thinking with a happy formula. From where does this vast realm of speculation arise if not from the freedom which each Jew assumes to have not only with the text that is present, but also with texts that have as yet not been revealed? The poet spoke of the journey from the desert to the book, meaning also the journey from the book to the desert. He also spoke of the question and the answer, of a dialogue where violence opened new directions of thought, crushed answers, and gave new horizons to those courageous enough to struggle for the question that always lives within the question, and the answer awaiting to be given a new answer.

We know that the Jew can never cease being a Jew. The decision is taken from him by inheritance and the world. The Jew is therefore forced to be constantly turned toward himself, questioning the meaning of his existence. Jabès noted that "the Jew has always been at the origin of a double questioning: questioning himself and questioning 'the other.' In truth, there is no avoiding this. As he is never allowed the ability to cease being Jewish, he is forced to ask the question of his identity. Hence he is, from the start, confronted with the discourse of *'the other'* and often his own life depends on it."[9]

We assume that we know the path of our destiny. The prophets have dreamed dreams, and Israel has experienced what it means to dwell alone, but we never learn these things, they are not facts, they are speculations. We speculate, hover over a text, find comfort in a psalm or in the life of another human, but this is never enough. We are children of the question. There is no authority to tell us that our speculations are dangerous and must be suppressed. We are wanderers through the desert and the city, through enemies and defamers, through the Holocaust and terrorism. Wherever we dwell, others rise up against us and become our accusers. We are the children of a desert God who gives vague answers to our appeals for guidance. He tests our courage and endurance.

We find pain and patience in the eternal Job who embraces and entices us. Where is the path that will enlighten us and show us a way? Jabès told us that "it must each time be discovered anew. A blank sheet is full of paths. You know you must go from left to right. You know there will be much walking, much effort. And always from left to right. You also know beforehand (at least sometimes) that once the page is black with signs you will tear it up. You will walk the same way ten times, a hundred times; the pathway of your forehead, and of your soul. All these ways have their own ways. Else they would not be ways."[10]

There are in fact many paths and each is a risk. The moment we open a book, we take a risk. We see the words and the spaces between the words, those that are not yet written but have been spoken. Reading and writing are risks. If we wish to avoid the risk, we no longer read or write, we follow and repeat what we have been taught. I think and write because I want to risk the confrontation of my thought with others. But I know that every book I write accompanies one that is not written and should be. This is the risk. The unwritten book will forever be the unwritten book. "The unwritten book," Jabès stated, "both enigmatic and revealing always slips away. And yet, only the reader's intuitive grasp of it enables him to approach the book's true dimension, this intuition enables him to judge if the writer has indeed come close to, or, to the contrary, has wandered from the book he had the ambition to write."[11]

---

[9]Ibid., 77.
[10]*The Book of Questions*, vol. I, 54.
[11]*From the Desert to the Book*, 82.

The book becomes a tear in the soul which we cannot heal. It forces us to strive to write the book we can never write. The book already exists. We, nevertheless, are driven to write the book of totality, the book that becomes idolatry, the book that is *the* answer to the questions we ceaselessly pose. The mystics dreamed of the book that has not been soiled by its earthly form, that radiates the perfection of divinity. The mystics knew that the book belonged to God; it was with God and God was the book. Radically different is the man who longs to write the book, who believes that it is within the human capacity to create the total book. Man knows that such a book could be nothing other than the idolatry of the mind, a demonic exaggeration of the human capacity. Man in his prudence withdraws from such a book. He turns in dreams to the unspoiled and total book which dwells in the heavens and is the book of divine light.

We could say with Jabès "that the Bible is the very opposite of the Mallarméan [the poet Mallarmé] book, given that nobody had conceived of writing it in the form in which we know it. It is an accumulation of texts – of books – of which nobody – and for good reason – could master the general plan. The books of the Bible mutually extend each other, meet head on at times, which is what creates their fantastic openness and, no doubt, also many of the questions they generate."[12] Jabès noted that interrogation of the book was at the core of his work. But the interrogation is in itself the writing of the book. In the absence of the book Jabès writes the book. The book is a metaphor which is the source of the dream, the poetic reverie which accompanies every page of the written text. The dream imagines the words that reveal the truth of the Word, which tells of the creative act which brought the universe into existence, which set forth the journey of Israel and spoke of its message to the world. The Word spoke in many forms and to many purposes, and messages came to many faiths. We listen to Jabès's words as they flow around Israel. We think of the poets of Christianity and Islam discovering the messages which the Word brought into the world. From each message came the longing for the book, and the longing remained the force that drove the spirit toward the hope of completion, but there was always the fear that completion is idolatry, more to be feared than any other reality. Idolatry lives close to the longing for the book. The line was thin and delicate that separated the latter from the worshipped idol, from the unrelenting orthodoxy that smothers and kills the spirit, claiming to be, and to know, the book. Orthodoxy knows that the spirit must die in order for the word to be deified.

---

[12]Ibid., 83-84.

In a letter to Verlaine, Mallarmé spoke of an "architectural and premeditated book and not a collection of chance inspirations, no matter how marvelous they may be, a book convinced that there exists only one."[13] Citing this text, Marcel Cohen asked Jabès to comment, assuming that he did not agree with Mallarmé. Jabès replied: "This last book would thus be the first, though always unbroached. It is no doubt the premonition of this book which gives its unity to my books, as if the architecture and the meaning of the book were never more than its physical and metaphysical approach."[14] There is little doubt that Jabès is a believing poet. His faith is rooted in the reality of the book, in its revelation and eternity. The world begins and ends in the book; it is the history of humankind, but also the reality redemption. "What in fact haunts me," Jabès stated, "is the last book, the one we will never write and which all our books try to look like, just as the universe in its becoming each day resembles a little more the pre-existing universe."[15] Again and again the dream of the poet turns to the book from which all other books emerge and in which they are submerged. The book that was before and will be after is the book which is the divine light in which our understanding finds light. The book is the primordial voice whose vocables speak of the Creation. The divine vocables, *I Am Who I Am — I Will Be Who I Will Be,* are those which no man can utter. Man is always negation, i.e., what he is not. Man says there is only Being, and Not Being is not. In man the negation is the reality of his existence. He is a state of becoming. His thinking begins in negation. The sacred text is read by the believer speaking to God, the unique One, while being embraced by his Holiness.

The reader comes to the text with devotion. This is what the reader is. He knows that only if he is inspired can he bear the text, be receptive to it. The reader is also a listener, and to listen he must be willing to hear, to be attuned to the words of the text. The poet speaks to a text which communicates with him.

The text is revealing. The text that is silent dies. The divine is present. "The infinite," Jabès said, "has the transparency of evil. Whatever goes beyond us despises us. Whatever escapes us destroys us."[16] We are startled by these words. We are aware of a peculiar human autonomy which has brought the divine within our dimensions, and we are told that evil lies in the infinite, in whatever escapes us. How can we believe that whatever remains within us is identifiable with truth? We see before

---

[13]Ibid., 84.
[14]Ibid., 84-85.
[15]Ibid., 84.
[16]*The Book of Questions,* vol. I, 56.

us the specter of truth dwelling in an earthly mold, but the divine has always been beyond this mold. It separated itself from human existence and it is in this rupture that the human dialogue begins. The beginning is always the question, and its shattering violence. We understand the poet better when we read his observation that "there comes a moment when the question collides with the question that shatters it. All that remains are shards of a question that cannot be formulated. Remorse of the question. Unappeasable torment of the answer." We speak of "the question that shatters" and the "unappeasable torment of the answer" and we are seized by "the storms which afflict man in his journey toward the divine. There is no ease nor harmony, no tranquil contemplation nor converse, there is thunder and earthquakes, disturbances of the soul, and the longing for quietude."[17]

We listen to a dialogue which Jabès put in *The Book of Questions:*

> My brothers turned to me and said: You are not Jewish. You do not go to the synagogue.
>
> I turned to my brothers and answered: I carry the synagogue within me.
>
> My brothers turned to me and said: You are not Jewish. You do not pray.
>
> I turned to my brothers and answered: Prayer is my backbone and my blood.
>
> My brothers turned to me and said: The rabbis you quote are charlatans. Did they ever exist? And you feed on their ungodly words.
>
> I turned to my brothers and answered: The rabbis I quote are beacons of my memory. One can only remember oneself. And you know that the soul has words as petals.
>
> The most thoughtful of my brothers turned to me and said: If you make no difference between a Jew and a non-Jew, are you, in fact, still a Jew?[18]

The dialogue is disturbing because the questions molest our answers. We have our answers and would like to have them undisturbed, but the poet nudges us, and forces us to rethink our answers. We do not want them shattered, but they can be if we think seriously about our questions. We hear the words which ask us about the meaning of being a Jew, we hear these same words about being a poet, a philosopher, or a scientist, but these latter words are easier to comprehend. Being a Jew makes us think about a common tradition and ways of living. We are

---

[17]*From the Desert to the Book*, 86.
[18]*The Book of Questions*, vol. I, 60-61.

Jews because we have taken the same journeys as others, heard the same texts and joined together for the same rituals. We have also turned to our fellowmen and sought to understand their lives, and the humanity which flows through them. We are Jews because of a common heritage, but we are also Jews because of the brotherhood we have longed for with all peoples. These are vague terms, easily enunciated, but they are also profound ones that are the sources of our dreams. From these dreams we form our visions of goals. We know that we are listening and we are giving. Brotherhood is both listening and giving, i.e., making the effort to consider who the other is.

Jabès spoke of his belief in the writer's responsibility. "I believe," he said, "in the writer's mission. He receives it from the word, which carries its suffering and its hope within it. He questions the words which question him. He accompanies the words which accompany him. The intuitive is shared as if spontaneous. Being useful to them (in using them) he gives a deep sense to his life and to theirs, from which his own has sprung."[19] This love of the word is the love of freedom. It is man's way either to the realm of the abstract or to that of history. But there is no abstract realm without the practical and the historical. We think of the word that has come to us from the generations and we realize that it is cloaked in man's historical existence. The word lives in history. It is the word of history, its embodiment and revelation. Jabès spoke of the journey from the desert to the book, thus the journey of a people with a message which belonged to history because it lived in and beyond history. History is the foundation of the message. God left his Word in history. He left man the freedom to choose the direction of his dialogue with words which reflect the Word. The freedom which man has to dialogue with the text, his unceasing commentaries which suppress one perspective to bring forth another bear witness to man's creative work, to his ceaseless reflection upon existence.

Man views his work as a constant reading of words that lie behind words, a reading of the silent words. His commentaries embrace not only the words he sees and hears, but also those that are unseen and unheard. "Every commentary," Jabès reminded us, "is first of all a commentary on a silence. To read the words behind the words – the decipherment of the book is infinite – can happen only through a violation. It consists, in a way, in violating the untouchable name of God."[20] Why are we so deeply concerned with the words behind words, if we are children only of our intellects, of the empiricism or abstractions that emerge from it? But there is an eternal Word that surpasses all the achievements of mind and

---

[19]Ibid., 58.
[20]*From the Desert to the Book*, 102.

practice. "The book," Jabès stated, "is always the beyond of speech, the place where it dies."[21] This belief in the book is the accomplishment of the Jew. His affirmation of eternity in time and space is the journey from the desert to the book. Each journey is a path toward the book, a road from time and space to the eternal. The presence of the eternal made it possible for us to become its creatures. We are its children, men and women created by the divine presence. We are its creatures not only in his presence, but also in his absence. The Jew is a man obsessed with the book.

Marcel Cohen reminded Jabès of something he had said earlier in *Return to the Book:* "One pebble discovered another and said: 'I see myself!' And then, 'Who has split me off from myself? Will we someday be a single pebble?'"[22] We experience our existence in rupture. We experience thought in both absence and negation. We struggle to overcome the separation we feel in thought and action. From book to book we are aware of the journey to the book. We seek to unite thinking and doing. We seek to reveal the silent words which embrace the world and human existence. We live and search for answers, hiding in the shells of hedonism. Our endurance is thin. We surrender easily to ideologies and traditions that deny the question and deify the answer. While our endurance is with us, we refuse the answer, and we become even more aware of how difficult it is to overcome negation and absence. They become the powers of all writing. Without their reality writing dies. We know that in separation we penetrate even more deeply the divine-human dialogue. We realize that there is no sinless existence. We remain the children of both Abel and Cain. There is no redemption in existence. There is no reconciliation in writing. There is only the increasing pains of negation, the pains of love. We do not surrender the pen. It is our only way to glimpse the divine, to feel the creative word. With mercy the divine preserves the distance between himself and his creature. The silence of words causes us to realize how dependent we are upon the community of humankind and how profoundly men are united in this search for the *yet to be revealed.*

"Writing," Jabès revealed, "means having a passion for origins. It means trying to go down to the roots. The roots are always the beginning. Even in death, no doubt, a host of roots form the deepest root bottom. So writing does not mean stopping at the goal, but always going beyond."[23] The passion for origins is longing for the dialogue with God, for the commentary that emerges from dialogue, from the Word that is

---

[21]Ibid.
[22]Ibid., 104.
[23]*Return to the Book* vol. 3 (Middletown: Wesleyan University Press, 1977), 159.

never a commandment but always a relationship, the source of the never-ending commentary. In other words, man is a wanderer from commentary to commentary. We must accept the reality of our going from path to path, of relinquishing the comfort of the answer. We wander in search of the book, which is always there reminding us of the presence of eternity in the midst of our mortality. The wanderer has no fixed dwelling. He is a being of the roads. He is a historical being following the paths and roads that men have followed through the ages, knowing that goals will surpass goals, and books will be followed by books struggling to approach the unapproachable, wanting to find the divine hints and sparks that flow from divinity. The path of the wanderer is difficult and severe. There are the enticements of the idols, their pleasures, the promises of the earthly prophets and messiahs, the messianism that flowed from revolutions that sought and promised to change society without changing man. The traveler observes. He revolts against the suffering he sees and he knows that justice should dominate, but he, like his brothers, is the progeny of Cain. We are bearers of "the mark." We wander, knowing our origins and struggling against them. In writing we seek to expose the conditions of our lives, the painful history of our existence, the depths of the rupture which is life. As Reb Sahed said: "I am, the tree calls to the tree, and the pebble to the simple pebble."[24] But hearing these words, neither the tree nor the pebble often replies.

Jabès quoted a few lines from a work of Philo of Alexandria, *De Specialibus Legibus*: "'Do not then entertain the hope ever to be able to apprehend me [God] or any of my powers in essence. But of what is attainable, as I have said, I readily and willingly grant you [Moses] a share, which means that I invite you to contemplate the universe and its contents – only let there be a continuous and constant longing for wisdom, which fills its devotees and disciples with glorious doctrines of exceeding loveliness.' When Moses heard this, he did not cease from his desire, but kept kindling his yearning for the invisible."[25] It is the invisible which is the object of love, which is always the beyond of experience and what surpasses the given. The question draws us toward the invisible; it journeys from question to question. It overcomes what it must surpass. Every question becomes empty in response to the question which follows; every word that is written becomes a path to the words of silence. Our love for the invisible makes it possible for us to see in every visible form a reflection of another. The visible form is the source of the

---

[24]Ibid., 156.
[25]*De Specialibus Legibus*, 1.45-50, cited in *Philo of Alexandria* (New York: Paulist Press, 1981), 88.

dream, the poetic reverie in which forms give birth to forms as dreams bring forth dreams.

> And Reb Fehad told this story:
>
> I mingled with a crowd of people and I asked: Where is the book?
>
> A man in the crowd replied: I had it in my hands.
>
> I went up to him and I asked: Show me the book.
>
> The man laughed and said: I threw it into the river so the water could read it.
>
> Then I said: Earth furnished the pages, water and fire the writing.
>
> Alas, the man was gone.
>
> And Reb Askol explained: Both of you were words in the book.[26]

Now I realized what I knew in the beginning: "The Word of God is not a commandment but a correspondence."[27] I knew that God is absent. All presence is limited to itself. I knew other things, but they have not yet come to know me. I await at the door of the silent word, listening to the sounds that hopefully will be words.

---

[26]*Return to the Book,* 147.
[27]Ibid., 162.

3

Surprise and Wonder:
The Journey to the Unexpected

I moved slowly from fascination with the system builders to the masters of the aphorism. There is Hegel and Marx and then Nietzsche and Kafka. The wonders of the embracing powers of thought confront the images of the aphorism. White fades into black, the letters and words multiply unendingly, and we feel man's unquenchable desire to be encompassing. Suddenly there is a reversal and the white not only resists the black, but it forces it to retreat. Man puts aside the encompassing systems and forges dialogues and listens to the aphorisms, the allegories, and the parables. The poet faces the philosopher and seeks to reveal the force of his existence, his visions and dreams. Man is no longer smothered in grandiose systems. He is freed to think and imagine with the aphorism. The aphorism shows him a direction, a possibility among many, and he must determine the path of his venture. A few black letters and then the whiteness of the labyrinth. But rarely do we find the aphorism suitable for our quest for certainty. The system eagerly shows us the way, revealing the laws of necessity and brushing away the contingencies that scatter doubts and blur the vision. With Jabès, we traveled with the aphorist, the poet of paradoxes and parables. Questions abound. Answers cleave to them for survival, but the questions reject them, force them to flee. The answers are ever present, but they are unable to force their reality upon the questions. The poet creates his dialogues. We become more and more aware how deeply life tears apart the created and necessary relationship between questions and answers, how deeply it forges more and more space for accidents and contingencies. What had become the dread of some philosophers, the power of contingency, became the joyful knowledge of others. Life seems more comfortable with the poet of paradoxes, with his aphorisms and tales. The poet leads us to dwellings that are open and airy, that show varied directions, that look both above and below. The dwellings have no walls. They are created by dreams and sensitivities. We can only imagine walls that are not walls.

"If you burn a book," the poet said, "it opens unto absence in the flame. If you drown it, it unfolds with the wave. If you bury it, it quenches the thirst of the desert. Because all words are pure water of salvation."[1] When the flame touches the book, its material reality becomes ashes, but like the phoenix, the ashes give birth to a new book, to what the poet called the book of absence. The book is now present in its absence, but it is no longer the original book. The book became ashes, and has now become absence. The book defies definition. We don't know and have never known what is the book. We only know that a book has given birth to books, that the words are not lost. They are the words of memory. They are presences in the present. The book cannot be destroyed. It unfolds if you drown it, and if you hide or bury it, it nurtures the lands about it. The book bears in it the words of salvation. Words are the source of life. With them we create the reality in which we live, in which we struggle to grasp the meaning of our existence, the wonders of our imagination and the limits of their possibilities. The book is our most precious creation. In it we have recorded our doings, the thoughts which have produced our civilization. The book has our commentaries and dialogues. The book is incomplete. From the book comes books. Each book leaves open spaces and vast new lands for us to explore. With the book, we discover the realms of written words, but also those of the unwritten, those which belong to the future, to our dreams.

In the fore-speech to *Yaël*, the fourth volume of *The Book of Questions*, we listen to these words: "I say; I am death, and forthwith am before God was. If we spurn God's image, do we not reject creation? Then where is truth but in the burning space between one letter and the next? Thus the book is first read outside its limits."[2] Truth lives in whiteness which has not found letters to occupy it. Truth lies in what has not been said, but will be said. The whiteness will always be where there are letters. What we tell leaves much to be told. We often wonder if Jabès is a storyteller, if he relates a time bound or timeless narrative. We wonder. Jews have always told the stories of their exiled lives in villages and towns, have created humorous and tragic personalities and situations which have become characteristic of their world of imagination. Jabès is not a storyteller in that tradition. His story is the tale of all stories. It is the story of the human experience, a spiritual tale of a poet attempting to

---

[1]*The Book of Questions*, vols. IV, V, V:29.
[2]Ibid., 7.

reveal the meaning of Jewishness, attempting to explore the exile of man from God, and of God from man. Jabès is a poetic wanderer of the desert, a man of visions that are always in and above life. Unlike the storyteller of the shtetl, the kibbutz, or the modern city, Jabès journeys through the generations, in and beyond time and space. This beyond is in time and space, a belonging that surpasses belonging, a being that is beyond being. Here the infinite and the finite touch with subtlety and delicacy. Nothing is fixed with a permanency which defies transparency. This is the realm of metaphor and metamorphosis. Life is a transfiguration of forms. The formless takes on form only again to emerge into the formless. From the phoenix images arise from images. Whatever is given, is given to death. Death hides life as life struggles to obscure death.

Writing is sometimes more than we intend, often it is less. In writing, the struggle lies between what is said and what is not said, between the text and the margins, between the whiteness of the page and the blackness of the letters. A deeper conflict lies between the aphorism and the concept that joins the forms of understanding to each other. "Writing a book," Jabès reminded us, "means joining your voice with the virtual voices of the margins. It means listening to the letters swimming in the ink like twenty-six blind fish before they are born for our eyes, that is to say, before they are fixed in their last cry of love. Then I shall have said what I had to say and what every page already knew. This is why the aphorism is the deepest expression of the book. It lets the margins breathe. It bears inside it the breath of the book and expresses the universe at the same time."[3]

We exaggerate when we say that each aphorism is the possibility of a book; we don't when we say that the aphorism permits us to enter a realm of thought which proceeds from our imagination, from images emerging from images. The margins are wide, the whiteness plentiful, and we can roam in many directions, searching for paths of travel. We are free to turn back again and again to the aphorism, to the others that gather around it, and seek for the images they arouse in us, for the thoughts they call forth. We leap from aphorism to aphorism, and suddenly we stop. The voice in the one links us to the voice in the other. One becomes a signal, an opening through which we see and hear the sounds, the words, of the others. Writing has become the wonder of voices speaking to each other with unexpected and unknown thoughts. We have created a dialogue and a commentary. The known and the unknown, the expected and the unexpected speak to each other in freedom. We discover that we are part of a dialogue, conscious of an unawareness which carries us from one level of imagery to another. We

---

[3]Ibid., 36.

learn to travel with the aphorism as we learn to value its companionship like a friend.

"A wise man (an adept of Hassidism disowned by the members of his community) taught me to doubt words because – this is my interpretation – syllables are enslaved and only a part of the truth which vainly tries to be true. Elsewhere this wise man praised as virtue the song of hope that rises out of the silence of words. But how come these joyful songs have such a strain of sadness they sound like sobs? It is because they are songs of dead words, eternal words which we humans cannot hear."[4] The companionship of words is difficult to maintain. Words embody both the absence and presence of truth. Man uses them to reveal and obscure the reality he intends for them. Man conceals and reveals the truths he seeks to express, but man himself is both presence and absence. In truth he would no longer be man; truth would be his silence. In falsity man would no longer be man; he would fade away into chaos. Joy and sadness, like truth and nontruth, belong to the same reality, but not in the way that one element melts into another and fades away. The elements relate to each by being bound to each other. They call each other forth, reveal their dependence upon each other. They belong consciously to each other. In belonging to each other, their presence becomes their absence and their absence is their presence. We listen to words not merely to repeat them. They are veils which reveal and obscure. We listen to words to hear what they say, what is their silence. We hear both the silence and the voice of words. The poet led us through his world of images, making us sensitive to what we see and what we hear. With this sensitivity, we followed him. We no longer escape him.

There are always white borders. Jabès gave us realms of possibility. No poetic tales are complete in their incompleteness, revealing in their nonrevelation. He remarked that "the word of the book comes from the white borders which the universe sustains with its mastery of the deep."[5] No longer are we treated to the rhythms of short stories and the embracing scenery of the novel. We learned to write with the poet. He left us room for our pens. He filled only a share of space. We were invited to enjoy the rest. At times what he said was obscure and we turned away in despair, but our thinking revealed a clarity which made it possible to turn back and grasp what was obscure and hidden. We are always turning back, rereading the beginnings. We discover how full they are with truth, and how pale they were when they first appeared to us. The whiteness of the borders entices us. There is so much more to be

---

[4]Ibid., 36-37.
[5]Ibid., 36.

said, so much is yet to be revealed. Jabès enticed us. He refused to create disciples. He needed companions. We discovered this as we traveled with him from imagery to imagery. He is like the phoenix, perishing before us and arising again in new forms.

"The desert," Jabès told us, "scorning distance reveals any presence of man or beast to the ear of the nomad who sleeps on the sand. Thus the book brings the world into view through our hearing step by step, and as if coming out of silence."[6] Truth appears to us in hints and traces. Even the book is heard only faintly and in spurts. The book is a mystery and a wonder, a mystery because it cannot be fathomed, and if it could be, it would no longer be the book. The book is a wonder because it is an introduction to the mystery of man's relationship to God. The book has been our companion for the generations. We have learned to ponder our unquenchable longing for truth, learned to find it intricately tied to contradiction, seeking to emerge from it, but remaining deeply dependent on it. We read. We listen attentively and sensitively to the traces of truth which, like sparks, arise here and there before us. We hold on to the aphorism with tenderness and gentility. We know that much is yet to be heard and seen. We are servants of the book.

We read with care Jabès's words: "The writer who declares himself a novelist or storyteller does not serve the book; he does not care about it for one moment and even considers it less than nothing. A novel is the writer's triumph over the book, and not the opposite, because the novelist makes a strong entrance with his characters and, with them as go-betweens, gives free rein to his innumerable voices. The book is trampled by them, its voice choked by them."[7] The novelist, like philosophical system builders, leaves little room for the aphorism. It would not be unfair to compare the modern system builders to novelists. These men embrace, encompass, and control the book; they are builders and architects of the mind they have captured. We dwell in these structures, admire their skillful artistry, and feel sheltered from the storms of doubt. They bear witness to the orthodoxy of the "set table," where questions find answers, and contingencies and doubts are exiled as the mind converts them into necessary moments of the logic of the spirit. We are painfully aware that the aphorism has disappeared in the believer, the whiteness has been blackened. Explanation, comprehension, and explication have overcome and surpassed the unknown, the unexpected, and the unclear. The novel, like the law of necessity, gives the fullness, the completeness, and the sense of totality which modern man seeks with avidity and intensity. The aphorism fades away, crushed

---

[6]Ibid.
[7]Ibid., 35-36.

and trampled by the triumphs of the fixed world of the novel. Nothing pleases the novelist more profoundly than his victory over the aphorism. The book is never there; it is always being created. The poet is the servant of the book, knowing that its existence is the source of his reality. He writes from and toward the book, the invisible reality which defies and limits the visible.

"I now believe," Jabès stated, "(and I have come to see this as a truth on which of a book's reality depends), I now believe that narrative in the usual sense, is not the business of the book, that it is extraneous to the book."[8] How odd and provoking are these words. The narrative pleases us, we hear the histories and tales of our past, we see our presence in them. We are embedded in the order of their development. We are fascinated by events, adventures, changes, and unexpected conclusions. We are addicted to the narrative. It reveals the self; it is the source of our explanations and definitions. The narrative is the medicine of the soul. Spoken in an orderly manner, it conveys rationality and clarity. Spoken with confusion, it points to disorder and unclarity. But the poet told us that the narrative is not the business of the book. With hesitation, we begin to approach him and attempt to grasp his words. The book is beyond the narrative. Its presence makes us aware that the narrative can only be the story, a moment of the book. The book is the source of all narratives. We cannot imagine a narrative that would be identical with the book. Where there is the book, there are narratives. Where there are narratives, the book is not necessarily present. The writer who seeks to identify the book and the narrative believes he has told the story of stories. The philosopher who assumes he has interpreted the nature of human history in such a way that history and thought unite has destroyed man's mortality and freedom. No figures are more perilous to human existence than those who have reduced the book to either a narrative, a novel, or philosophic dialectics.

"You are a storyteller, a friend said to me one day. How can I be when words and images always cut in and want to be heard with their own aura, when the story is built out of bits of counter-stories, and when silence lies in wait for the world?"[9] Jabès did have a story to tell, a narrative of escape, of exile, of solitude, of family, and of Jewishness, but this story was absorbed in the epic of the book. Jabès wrote the odyssey of a wandering people inseparable from the book which accompanies them from desert to lands and peoples, where they dwell as exiles. No longer the story of man, a crew, and an awaiting wife and son, this odyssey bears in it the divine presence and the commentaries which have

---

[8]Ibid., 35.
[9]Ibid., 115.

been written through the generations in response to a wandering tribe attempting to comprehend how it should live in exile, and for what purpose. Stories belong to this epic, but they are not to be identified with it. Jabès is the epic poet. The poetry of the epic embraces what is said and what is not said, what is spoken in the commentaries and what is constantly breaking into the commentaries, or hovering over them. The epic goes beyond the dimensions of the story. It gives the story place and time, and surpasses it. Life and death relate to each other in a similar way. The living is only a moment emerging from death and returning to it, giving the ages the words and deeds of men which death submerged at every moment. The book alone remains beyond the grasp of death.

Jabès remarked with piercing insight that "you never lose the book: you lose yourself."[10] The odyssey of the book hovers over the activities of men and women; it is beyond the figures we call our Fathers and our Teacher. It is beyond the Prophets. The epic belongs to the eternal wandering of the book. Jabès's epic is spiritually incomplete; it is the most ancient and most contemporary of all epics. It has no beginning. It has no end. It was with God before the creation; it belonged to the people before they knew of the book; it contained their visions and sufferings before they had visions and dreamed dreams. It was not an epic of wars, heroes, and the founding of empires. It was not the epic of the battle between Satan and God. It was the epic of a book. "The book," Jabès said, "does not need man to come into being. It does so through him. As in our lives we are forever pushed by the hours one after the other. A book which could have held all the words for our thoughts and gestures, but which definitely kept only those it chose to make common cause with in their order and economy."[11] The book makes it impossible for us to deify any human experience. It saves our humanity.

We imagine the book as the dwelling of the light which illumines all that is in it, drawing it toward the clarity and obscurity of the aphorism. The book is, at the same time, the idea of the book. The book bears within it the light by which we see ourselves. God is inseparable from the book. He is the book illuminating the book. Man is the vehicle through which the book is revealed to both man and world. But man remains an impure vehicle of illumination. He reveals the book as a commentary. The book is the history of commentaries and for this history the rabbis seek not only discussions but also aphorisms. The wonders of the rabbis are the lights which are embodied in their aphorisms. Heroically and stubbornly the rabbis maintain their interpretations as they wander with the people from lands to lands, suffering with them the scorn of neighbors and the

---

[10]Ibid., 114.
[11]Ibid.

suspicions of other faiths. The people want to be like their neighbors, but they cannot escape the book which like a cloud encompasses them. It is the same cloud that accompanied the generations before us, the cloud of the hidden God. In the people's lives we find ours, in their responses we seek to mold the ones which we make and will make.

"The walker," Jabès stated, "dissolves into his journey. Years are towlines carried off by the current. The ground is suddenly no longer solid where the rose bends to look at itself. So little water. So much. Thirst performs the miracle of giving the world the privilege of dreams. To drink. To drink the air, the dark, the day."[12] We think of a journey which goes in search of a walker, and we think of a walker who has become his journey. In whatever direction we turn, we see that man and his journey belong to each other. The journey is no longer the road from here to there, from means to ends. The journey is a ballet of forms. It is both horizontal and vertical. The journey goes forward and backward. It begins in the beginning, but the beginning is always beyond beginnings. The journey commences in the labyrinth. In the poetic reverie images create images. The journey is created with thirst, the longing for the unknown, for the nothingness which is the source of reality, for the remembrance which lives in reality giving it limitation and mortality. The thirst is the love of the invisible, the dream which becomes dreams, the vision from which visions emerge, and to which they return. The journey belongs to the book. Man journeys because of the book, the book of infinite journeys. Without the book, man's dwelling belongs only to the world. The book causes him to look upward and wonder about the foods which descend from the heavens.

But what is the book of which we have spoken from page to page? The book has no definition. If it did find one, it would not be the book, but an infinitesimally small moment of the book. But in the infinitesimally small there is a quality of the book, a moment of creativity and beauty. If our question is directed to the book, probing its nature, its structure, and its form, then the answers we elicit are unclear, vague, and arbitrary. We are, however, not dismayed by the answers. The lack of definition, of preciseness, and of completeness indicates that the book is the beginning of beginnings, the abyss from which reality emerges and returns. The book is the foundation of foundations. We can describe the book only with paradoxes and parables, but we come no closer to the book than to the miracle which comes to us from life, from the act of creativity which remains both incomprehensible and boundless. The miracle is the book, its eternal presence is in its absence. We are drawn to the book because we are able to move from it. The book embraces us. It

---

[12]Ibid., 58.

leaves us naked. We grasp the reality of solitude from the book. The book creates books, as it brings forth commentaries and dialogues. We are interpreters in all that we do spiritually. The book is the spirit. It is the word. In the spirit and the word all that is creative is embraced. In the arts and sciences, we reveal the powers of spirit and word which lie in the eternal presence of the book. We stand before the book in all that we do and speak. The book was given in the beginning. The history of humanity is its discovery. This is the revelation of the book.

The poet observed that "a life without miracles is doomed to the dullness of stagnant water. It has the dragonfly's capers to wake it. On a different, but equally reduced plane, dust knows from birth the fuel of downtrodden old age. Rejected, it only irks our itinerary. Exile is its rest."[13] Another poet, Octavio Paz, said in his Nobel Prize address that two words *thank you,* have been from the dawn of humanity spoken by men. *Thank you* is an expression of gratitude for a grace extended from either God to man or from man to man. "Grace," Paz noted, "is a gift. The person who receives it, the favored one, is grateful and if he is not base, he expresses his gratitude."[14] Jabès speaks of the miracle; Paz of *gracia,* or grace. Both speak of the miracle which gives man the capacity to redeem himself from the limits placed upon him by his animality and his practicality. Grace is the added reality, the redeeming power which gives man the new perspective, the unexpected possibility, allowing him to surpass the senses. The miracle lies neither in this, nor in that, act and event. The miracle lies everywhere that man recognizes in gratitude the grace of the undefinable imagination. This recognition is the realization of the presence of the unknown, a presence that is the source of man's thoughts and acts. This presence is the cause of man's gratitude, a thank you for the powers which allow him to overcome the repetitive and necessary qualities of human life. There are the foods which come from the earth. There are those which come from the heavens. Man looks down, but also ahead and upward. What comes to us from above is of equal significance that which comes to us from below. To say thank you is more than a gratitude for a particular act or insight; it is the expression of an awareness that life, although it is pain and hardship, is also spiritual exploration and excitement. Life belongs not only to nature, but also to divinity. There is no answer to the miracle of life, there are questions exploring and discovering the unknown which lies in it.

Again and again the poet spoke of the death of God, and we hear these words and wonder about their meaning. They are difficult words

---

[13]Ibid.
[14]*In Search of the Present, Nobel Lecture, 1990* (San Diego: Harcourt Brace Jovanovich, 1990), 3.

to hear and even more difficult to enunciate. They strike defiantly at our traditions, the beliefs of our Fathers, the commentaries of the rabbis, but they are present and we hear their reverberations. How do we relate death to God? He cannot die like a mortal, for if he could, he would only be an idol. God is absence, but this absence is a permeating reality. His absence is his presence in life and world. The world left to the dialectics of nature, to the laws of necessity, to those who devour contingency and possibility, is one in which logic absorbs rhetoric and divinity finds its demise. The poet spoke of the death of God. He remarked:

> The tree of knowledge bore wormy fruit. Did God know this?
>
> Adam ate the apple with its acid taste of defiance,
>
> Henceforth he would live and die by fighting against
>
> God, by relentlessly struggling with himself.

The fruit which Adam ate was wormy; to have eaten the fruit of perfection would have made Adam into God. It would have destroyed the possibility of human history. There could be no Cain and no Abel, no Saul and no David. Without the jealousies and rages of men there would be no law, no ethics, and no dreams of peace. The worm in the fruit made human history possible. Man needed to discover how much of the fruit he could save from the worm, how much the worm saved for him. The struggle to preserve the fruit is the human task, the extent of its preservation is man's miracle, the grace that abides in human life.

The poet continued:

> You loathed Him who created the mortal world for you and who, to help you live, hides you from yourself.
>
> The universe belongs to him who survives it.
>
> In that respect, the lie is our greatest blessing.
>
> You reject what consoles you, O fool, you will suffer more than God if He exists. For truth is the mirage of a summit which our mountains point toward.[15]

The reality of the divine existence lies in man's struggle to turn from God, to be in opposition to him, to save himself through the lie. Man doesn't need philosophical speculations to prove the divine existence; he requires only a careful awareness of his desire to be like God, or his desire to deny him through the lie. In whatever direction we follow, if we affirm his majesty or deny his reality, we are involved in his reality. Man is theomorphic. We hide from God and we hear the question: Where art thou? We confront him and remain in conflict with him. We can become

---

[15]*The Book of Questions* vol. IV, 60.

his servant and destroy our humanity. We can deify our humanity and suppress his holiness and truth. We go in all these directions. In one period of life we find our atheism, in another we discover our dependence; in one we act with spontaneous freedom, in another we explore the realms of receptivity. We storm the heavens to seize the divine light. We find it incompatible with our mortality. We sing praises to our dignity while we harbor the forces of its destruction. We lie about our goodness. We distort the hopes and consolations which trust has always made possible for us. Trust remains the summit from whose vision we imagine a new covenant between man and God. The summit is the vision from which we envision the death of God.

"Being born," Jabès said, "means looking for your name; finding it means you are dying."[16] In every man there is the question of the meaning of existence. In whatever direction he turns, whomever he confronts, questions of comparison and purpose emerge. Every morning and every evening, man faces the same dilemma. He hears the questions from those about him, from those whom he loves. The questions speak of direction and growth, activity and profession. Man needs to be named. He needs to be called a lawyer, a teacher, a businessman, an artist. This search for a name overwhelms his existence. From school to university, from one examination to another, from one level of experience to higher positions in the professional hierarchy, man is driven to acquire names, designations, and realms of admiration. Life becomes identical with the search for the name. The search is not clear; there are doubts which surround it and these increase in intensity as the search for the name continues. The doubts which hover about this search grow in number and depth as we become more and more identifiable with our search, our name, and our activity. But we are more than our name, more than our activity. We seek the name. We were required to name all things, but the search must always remain the search. The end of the search is death. To find the name makes it no longer possible for us to wonder, to dream dreams, to have visions. With the depths of our longings we go in pursuit of the name. There is, however, a deeper longing of which we are not always aware: the longing not to discover the name.

Man goes in search of the name, but man is more than the name. He is the being who gives names. Identification with the name limits man's right to wonder, to think beyond the name. Man needs to journey beyond every earthly achievement; the present is always a preparation for the future. Man is a being who is spiritually dissatisfied, who longs for what is yet to be, for the unknown and the unexpected. "Dawn," the poet observed, "is more than a hope, it is an elect full of fresh fervor.

---

[16]Ibid., 32.

Straining towards what is to come, his ties cut, man when he is finally free gorges himself on eternity. His gravity lies in being available and great, in the vacancy of a moment which will fuse with his life. Not to expect anything and yet to die daily of infinite expectation."[17]

Man's dissatisfaction is metaphysical. He is a being of forms and images. He is as much a thinker as a builder and producer. He creates and re-creates. He gives sound to sound, form to form, image to image. Restrict man to the cage of finite existence, you deprive him of his search for transcendence, his need to wonder. Dawn is the new beginning, the beginning which lies in the abyss of all beginnings. The beginning is the unknown act, a leap of novelty, the foundation for what is to follow, but neither assumed nor determined by it. We call it the possibility "of infinite expectation." What startles us about man's need to "gorge himself on eternity" is that in this need we discover that man is a metaphysical being, that life does not begin with the physical, but with the metaphysical. Reality lies in what can be thought, in the powers of the imagination, in the fullness of fervor, in the search for what is to come. With the slow death of this fervor, man is reduced to his feelings, his instinct, the immediacy of sight, hearing, touch. Deprive man of his metaphysical powers, and you deprive him of his humanity.

Death is a preoccupation which never left Jabès. He was a poet of life. He was a poet of death. These two realities forged the dialogues and commentaries which became the poetry of his reveries. "Death," he stated, "is the gratuitous act *par excellence*. Creating means imitating death which is God's daring and imagination. Death is in everything which will be tomorrow, so that man's quest of the absolute has to go through it."[18] Death is man's fate. It surrounds his life. Man is capable of deifying life, of giving to it a sense of totality, but death stands in the way. It is the eternal remembrance of man's mortality, of his oneness with time and space. Time is the limit to human existence. We have no possibility of surpassing time which is similar to space. Our mortality separates us from God. Man's quest is for the powers of creation, to live timelessly through the creative act. We struggle to negate the present, to bring forth the future. The phoenix is the image of man's attempts to find in death the source of life. Realities must die and be born again. We are always going "away from here," leaving a world of ashes and decay for the visions of tomorrow. This is not a disregard of the present, an arbitrariness which would make a mockery of the here and now. Such arbitrariness would lead to a disrespect for human life. We can only grasp the powers of life by living through them, honoring and admiring

---

[17]Ibid., 33.
[18]Ibid.

them. Death is the rejection of their deification, of the longing of men to find the absolute and impose it upon life. Death proclaims the mortality of life, of all things which emerge from it. When human creations appear to surpass their limitations, we seek to discover hints of the divine in them. We remain hesitant to ascribe them solely to human creativity. Death is the unveiling of human truth, as this same truth unveils the fate of death.

If death conditions life, then life finds in death the source of its undefinable and incomprehensible possibilities. Life can always see itself as surprise. Life becomes a surprise to itself. Circumscribed and embraced by death, life explores the infinite forces which constitute its existence. Man's mortality is the source of life's exuberance. Life that is surprised by life is a force that is radically defiant of death. "Surprise," the poet noted, "(letting yourself be surprised, becoming passive, reaching by and by a total receptivity) is the sap of creation and its pact. You cannot build on what you have already seen, already thought. But you see and think as you dig, as you build, as you complete. For completion is another beginning."[19]

Nothing creates greater enthusiasm than the feeling of surprise. Nothing lends greater joy to the act of creation than the surprise we feel about the magic and mystery which lie in it. Surprise is always accompanied by wonder. It can never leave the human experience without causing it to despair, to become frigidly constrained by its limitations, and to feel the power of necessity dominate and suffocate the wonders of visions and dreams. Surprise belongs to receptivity, or letting ourselves be surprised. The world must bear in it an excitement for us; its forms and relations, its colors and tones, its architecture and movements must be received with enjoyment. Where this joy is absent there is the passivity of indifference, there is the formality of distance in which we claim to find objectivity. Receptivity brings with it novelty and difference. It brings with it the unexpected and the unpredictable. Receptivity is an openness to the universal, to all the forms of human creativity, to the mystery and wonder of the creative act. The poet journeys with us to lands and peoples where there is an openness to imagery and forms. The feeling of surprise belongs to that openness which frees us from the dogmas of orthodoxies, from their deification of traditions and habits. Jabès is a poet of wonder and surprise. He is a poet of the desert, of changing forms and infinite tones.

"Becoming conscious of death," Jabès stated, "means denying any hierarchy of values which does not account for the stages of darkness when man is initiated into the mysteries of the night. Death is both the

---

[19]Ibid.

loss and the promise of a hope which day wears itself out courting at every moment. To be or not to be in the absurd agony of a secret glimmer until morning."[20] How can we contemplate "the stages of darkness" if we don't imagine those of light, if we don't imagine the birth of man as a new light? Death extinguishes light only to make room for the new birth. The intimacy of birth and death allow for continuity. Death is the foundation of life as life finds its fulfillment in death. But what are these "mysteries of the night"? We can only speak of them in paradoxes, in words which point to transfigurations and metamorphoses. Death and life are not separate realities. Death is alive in life, making it possible for man to speak of creativity as wonder. Creativity makes it possible for us to understand how realms of reality fade away as new forms emerge, absorbing the old and transforming them into different figurations. This wondrous conjunction of opposites, of light and darkness, of order and disorder, creates a sensitivity for the dialogues which we form with our fellowmen and the worlds they have brought forth. The sensitivity to growth and decay, to difference and habit, to beauty and disorder, to reason and the imagination, draws us toward the wonders of the human spirit.

The wonders of this spirit are no assurance of their continuity. We believe that in life death is a certainty, but an unpredictable and unexpected one. "The [man and the universe] will be destroyed in the moment they least expect it. Hence becoming conscious of death does not mean going straight towards it, but on the contrary, plunging into life to take on its ochre renewals."[21]

Jabès has taken us from one book of questions to another. The more we journey with him, the more we become aware of the imaginative powers which dwell in human life. Words burst forth in unexpected images, and from these images others emerge. We are more and more aware of the poetic reverie, of the liberation of the spirit from the shackles of morbid scholarship. Man without wonder loses his humanity. We repeat this often. It is the force which drives us toward those renewals which redeem life from death, which give life its joy, and which allow man to smile defiantly in spite of his most tragic adversity. No event in human life allows us to deify evil. The human spirit transcends every attempt to reduce life to the war of good and evil. In this war, man knows that the victory must be his. The victory is granted to him only in the presence of the book.

---

[20]Ibid., 34.
[21]Ibid.

4

Commentaries and Dialogues, Yukel and Sarah

"You chose," said Reb Eloda, "now you are at the mercy of your choice. But did you choose to be Jewish? And Reb Ildé: What is the difference between choosing and being chosen, since we cannot help submitting to choice?"[1] With the poet, we ponder the subtle movement that takes us from choice to chosenness, and we don't feel that we belong fully to either moment of reality. We belong to both, but do we belong equally to both or more to one or to the other? There are times we feel the powers of choice dominating our lives; at others, we feel the weight of being chosen, sharing a destiny with a community, having a history that not only was, but is always present. This is a history which we not only relate to ourselves, but one which the world constantly reminds us of. We tell our own history, and others tell it to us. We are history, a people identified with events which not only formed them, but never leave them, even if they walk in new directions. We feel different from other peoples, although we want to be among them. Often we hope to forget our history, we turn from the God who in his absence is always present. Why did we have to be created by a God and become his chosen? Perhaps we could comprehend absence, but would not this absence be a startling presence? The more we say about chosenness, the more we realize how little we have said. There is a mystery and a wonder in the relationship. It never lets us alone, and we can never be free of its reality.

Reb Midrash asked: "If we have been created to endure the same suffering, to be doomed to the same prearranged death, why give us lips, why eyes and voices, why souls and languages all different?"[2] We know

---

[1]*The Book of Questions I*, vol. I (Middletown: Weslyan University Press, 1970), 29.
[2]Ibid., 31.

that we can speak, that we are different from each other, that we are the children of many histories, and that we are creative in our differences. In them, we find the sources of our being, the individuality of our souls, the distinctness of our expressions, and the wonder of our thought. No matter what thoughts and movements we determine to be meaningful for us, we remain the voice of their clarity and significance. We are the masters of our words. They are our instruments. They serve our thinking. Often we have found that our words have become our captors and we have fallen into their prisons, doomed to worship their sounds and rhythms. We have struggled with our words and forced them to yield to the powers of thinking, guarding their separation from thought. Man never fails to realize how profound is the attempt of words to dominate thinking until he faces the imprisonment of words. This imprisonment he has seen with disturbing reality in the present world.

Jabès stated with startling clarity the identification of the book and life. "If God is," he said, "it is because He is in the book. If sages, saints, and prophets exist, if scholars and poets, men and insects exist, it is because their names are found in the book. The world exists because the book does. For existing means growing with your name. The book is the work of the book."[3] Do not these words imply a deification of the book? If we read again and again, we realize that the book is not a particular book. It is the book in and from which all books are written, and in which sages and prophets find and write their lines. The book is everything and it is nothing, i.e., the reality from which all things are born and to which they return. The book is not only the primal birth, but the continuing birth. It is always present, but the book is always absent. God is present in the book only in his absence. This absence is always beyond a particular commentary. The book is the revelation of revelations. The book is present in every revelation, but it is always absent. The absence of the book remains its presence. "It is the sun, which gives birth to the sea. It is the sea which reveals the earth. It is the earth which shapes man."[4]

From the book comes books, from every reality another emerges and finds its meaning and its purpose, but this only for the moment. In the next, other realities will appear and they will suppress and hide the ones that preceded. Only the book is forever present, all else comes and goes like the sands and forms of the desert. We live among these changes and have no control over them. They control us when we no longer think of them, when they carry us with them. We do think and we struggle to master these changes with words, making them part of our reality. We

---

[3]Ibid.
[4]Ibid., 32.

cannot live apart from the book in which we write about our existence, in which existence has always been recorded. Our belonging has not been our choice. We were chosen to be recorded in the books.

Yukel has never been at ease. He has always been here and elsewhere. He has always been in the past when he is in the present, and in the future, at the same time, he is in the present. Yukel is like the wandering sand and its ceaseless forms. Yukel has no home. Every presence is an absence to Yukel. Jabès spoke with moving and forceful words: "You have gone through dreams and through time. For those who see you (but they do not see you – I see you), you are a shape moving in the fog. Who are you, Yukel? Who are you, Yukel? Who will you be?"[5] These are the absurd questions which defy answers, which mock them and do violence to their certainty and self-assuredness. Yukel hovers over us, making us uneasy, he reminds us how alone we are in the desert when the book comes forth.

"Whosoever does not believe in the book," said Reb Gandour, "has lost faith in man and in the kingdom of man."[6] In the book, God allows man to speak of him. In the book man permits God to reveal himself. This is the intimate relationship that permeates the work of Jabès. His dialogic poetry, the poetry of question and answer, the poetry of speaking rabbis, draws together man's insatiable desire to think and imagine with the divine presence. We know little of this presence, and, in this not knowing, its reality becomes more and more real to man. "Is there, brother, a word dreamier and more alert, more miserable and more fraternal than the one you incarnate?"[7] The incarnated word bears in it a mystery. We cannot escape the fact that it is there in the book. We move around it, interpret it, but we always return to it. It defies our labors of understanding. It has become a fateful word and we accept it as such. We turn to the words that are gathered about it, and we attempt to embody it in them, but the word remains the word as the book remains the book. The people live in and from the book. Their persistence and courage in defense of the book have given them a history and a purpose. They live to preserve the book, and preservation for them is discussion and interpretation. They were born in the book and die in and with it.

Jabès spoke of our ties to beings and things and showed us their fragility. "A breath, a glance, a sign, and sometimes just a shadow such is, roughly, the original nature of our ties. If our ties are eternal, it is because they are divine." Reb Léca said, "You try to be free through writing. How wrong. Every word unveils another tie." And Reb Vita

---

[5]Ibid.
[6]Ibid., 36.
[7]Ibid.

added: "I name you. You were."[8] We feel as if we are encompassed by words, as if the divine has enclosed us in them. The more we interpret, the more we write. We discover the ties which bind us to all relationships. There is no freedom in writing, there is only the emerging of words from words, as thought is born in thought. Jabès introduced us to poetic wanderings and paths of interpretations, to the fate that embraces the Jew, the being devoted to the book. When man thinks and imagines, he encounters and confronts the book. Writing makes man aware of how dependent he is upon the word which is the opening to the words he has not yet heard, and has not imagined.

Let us listen to the commentaries of six rabbis. They are the imaginary commentators who lead man to dialogue. With them we begin to speak as we always speak when another has spoken and is speaking. If we speak, we listen, we need to hear the words which will create our words. Reb Ab's commentary begins with these words: "A writer's life takes its sense through what he says, what he writes, what can be handed down from generation to generation. What is remembered is sometimes only one phrase, one line. The writer steps aside for the work. The work depends on the reader."[9] The dialogue of writer and reader reveals that constant dialogue between truth and lie. The writer must be read, but reading is most often rewriting. The writer has lost dominance over what he has written. The writer is forced to leave the truth of what he has said to the lie, which the readers for generations have imagined he has said. The conflict between writer and reader is continuous. When we speak of truth and lie, we comprehend the struggle between falsity and truth. In this struggle, we become more and more aware of the rupture that exists between writing and reading. Rupture is the mark of human existence.

Reb Ab continued: "How can I show what I create, outside myself, page after page, when doubt erases every trace of my passage? How could I make you part of my adventure, when it is the avowal of my loneliness and of the road?"[10] This commentary, like all the others, embraces that movement of doubt and passage. Certainty has no place in the commentary, although we know that we are drawn to the commentary by the presence of the book. We write because it is a way of finding our path in the world, wanting to know if this path is determined or alive with doubts. The passage from one degree of understanding to another is never certain, but necessary. We move with the intention of certainty. We find shifting forms and perspectives. We seek

---

[8]Ibid., 37.
[9]Ibid., 39.
[10]Ibid., 40-41.

companionship and we discover loneliness. We search for a path of truth and we find the lie. The truth defies us. It appears to us like the chameleon. Its many colors attract us. We find that what we seek is, in truth, not what we will find. We know that we must travel and search for what can be discovered, but discovery is always an illusion; it gives lie to what we seek. The end of Reb Ab's commentary is loneliness and doubt, but in these we find the way of man who knows that where there is no doubt, there can be no truth. Truth cannot stand apart from doubt. Doubt is inseparable from truth. Reb Ab's thoughts affect us deeply. They leave us with no definitions and no certainties. Truth is embraced by doubt. Doubt is embraced in truth. Where one is alone, it loses its meaning and becomes distorted.

The commentary of Reb Ten spoke these poetic words: "After the road, and before the road, there are stones and ashes on scattered stones. The book rises out of the fire of the prophetic rose, from the screams of the sacrificed petals. Smoke, smoke for all who see only fire, who smell only dawn and death. But the order of summits, the order of ruins, is wedding gladness."[11] The road has borne witness to greatness and sadness. It goes through the desert and stands under the sky. The road has known pain and hope. The road has caused me to look skyward and envision my God embracing me. On the road, I look ahead and see the shapes of the shapeless desert. My road has taken me through internment camps, to the gulags, to concentration camps, and all the places man has invented to destroy and torture his fellowman. I am always on the road learning to suffer the sufferings of love. This road is the way of instruction which generations have followed to learn of sufferings which men endure to guard their God. The road is there, although not always visible; it fades away and comes forth again from the fire in which it is being consumed. The road challenges our strength and its endurance. This is the road on which the books are born, from which books emerge and tell their stories of burning chimneys and inextinguishable conflagration. The road is not only a remembrance of sights and images, it has gathered on to it the sounds of prophecy and despair, of love and frustration. The road is the witness to both life and death. It is never freed of the smoke which lazily floats around it. There is an intimacy between the ruins of the generations and the absence of God. The road has shown man how limited is his happiness upon earth. To be Jewish is to know with a mysterious intensity the road of faith and suffering. But the road doesn't weaken man. He grows in defiance and constancy of purpose. Never does God escape man's love. His absence only deepens it.

---

[11]Ibid., 41-42.

The commentary of Reb Zam was: "You enter the night, as a thread enters the needle, through an opening propitious or bloody, through the most luminous breach. Being both thread and needle, you enter the night as you enter yourself."[12] Commentaries are written upon commentaries and those which we write are only possibilities among possibilities. But each commentary in its way is a commentary for another. When we reflect upon what Reb Zam has said, we know his words have come forth from many others, as ours come forth from his and those that cluster about our words. The road leads through the mist of darkness and light. The road is not like other roads, it is the road of dialogue between man and God. Its path through the needle is narrow and painful. No longer is there arbitrariness. The road cannot wander at will, it is the road which bears a people who carry with them God. This God is the light of the universe which remains hidden in darkness. The needle carries its thread through the night of the universe. We know of the road that illumines the darkness; it's a road that goes not only through humankind, but through each of us. In the self there is the experience of the needle and the thread, of the absence and presence of the divine. Our daily life speaks of the unresolved contradictions of hope and despair. We long for the divine in a world where presence is absence, a world given over to necessity. We long for the divine within ourselves, where darkness is rarely set aside by the light. We live with contradictions, with the never-ending questions which ceaselessly shatter our answers. We go forward necessarily creating commentaries.

Reb Elar commented: "You can retrace a road in your mind or your veins. You can dig a road in men's eyes. The child is the master of roads. Descend. Melt and melt into the fall, oblivion, which is falling of things and beings. With the weight that has found its weight for dying."[13] Reb Elar's commentary seems obscure and we approach it with both hesitancy and wonder. What is Reb Elar attempting to tell us? Often when we ask this question, we find it to be inadequate. Reb Elar may be telling us nothing if we think of telling as if it is a bearer of information. Reb Elar tells us nothing. He brings to us images and dreams. His words send us on many paths. They open to us many commentaries with questions and their answers. Reb Elar asks us to imagine and to think, or to think and then to imagine, or simply to imagine in our thinking. We retrace a road in our mind, but there it will only be the road of thought. We retrace a road in our veins and there it will be the road of our blood, of the blood of humankind. This road belongs to our life as it stretches back through the generations. This road we don't see as we watch the

---

[12]Ibid., 42.
[13]Ibid., 43.

comings and goings of the world about us. We see this road in our inner life as men have seen it before us, and revealed it to us. This is the road we get from the past, from the history of the people. We struggle to be open to the road, but our thinking often stands in the way. It needs to explain. In the explanation, the road fades away. We have no way of coming to the road without the eyes of thought. The road remains always present, but it is ruptured.

For the moment, the rabbis have spoken. Yukel begins to speak: "I look for you. The world where I look for you is a world without trees. Nothing but empty streets, naked streets. The world where I look for you is a world open to other worlds without name, a world where you are not, where I look for you."[14] The rabbis comment on the book. It is present to them in its absence. In its presence, they would not have to comment upon it; they would not be rabbis. They are rabbis because they know how to bring the book back into the world, but only through commentary. Yukel speaks of a world where the book is not only absent, but is forgotten. Where there is the book, the world has a modicum of sanity, but what is the world without the book, how do we maintain our sanity in such a world, a world empty of dialogue, a world without values? In this world, we have lost relationship and love, the love which bound Yukel to Sarah. The book and its rabbis return the world to order, to the word and its struggle against violence. But even the book cannot put aside necessity, the ruler of the world.

Yukel continues to speak: "There are your steps, steps which I follow and wait for. I followed the slow road of your steps without shadow, unaware who I was, unaware where I went. One day, you will be there. Here, elsewhere, it will be a day like all the days when you are there. Perhaps tomorrow, to find you, I followed yet other bitter roads where salt broke salt."[15] In Yukel's voice, there is despair and pain, the lover without the beloved, the beloved without the lover. Yukel speaks for himself, and for the people who have lost the paths to their God. Their world is so obscure that they no longer see traces of him. Their eyes are dimmed, their sight watery and unclear. Men discovered the divine separated from his creation; a veil of melancholy hangs over it, a bitterness comes with every taste and every touch.

Yukel continues to speak, his pain and confusion have no end: "In the world where I look for you, you are both grass and ore. You are the scream lost where I lose my way. You are also where nothing wakes, oblivion with ashes of mirror."[16] These are shuddering words which

---

[14]Ibid.
[15]Ibid., 43-44.
[16]Ibid., 44.

open to us the darkness which man brings upon the earth, the screams of despair which reveal our loss of way. We are lost in the desert of humanity, among the billions who live what they call life. The veil of darkness comes upon the earth, but there is a flicker of light, there is Yukel who is in search of Sarah's scream, who remains stubborn and devoted. Yukel lives only as the unquenchable search for the light. We listen to the subtleties of the rabbinic commentaries, we hear the voices of the Talmud and the Kabbalah, and in these we find moments of peace. Yukel comes in the midst of the rabbinic conversations and brings the messages of despair and pain. The rabbis know the safety of the parted sea. They walk with trust on a road which leads to God. They are the believers where others find no belief.

Yukel came with the agony of his search, with the futility of his love, and the scream that came from the lost way. The commentary of Reb Dabes began with the line of tranquil faith: "The road which leads me to you is safe even when it runs into oceans."[17] In these few remarkable words, we hear again the cry of faith which arose from generation to generation. These words must be uttered. Without them, the despair would destroy man. This is the delicate dialectic between tragedy and faith, between madness and meaning. The powers of one support the forces of the other. Together they weave those irreconcilable contradictions into patterns of order where each element is bound to be related to the other. There are times when the powers of contradiction pull so fanatically against each other that we despair of their reconciliation.

Reb Elati remarked: "I am rhythm...without rhythm you would not see the sun every morning. You could not. Rhythm is internal. It is the rhythm of fate. No matter how you tried, you could neither go faster nor more slowly.... I went to God because God was my fate. I went to the word of God because the word of God was my fate."[18] Reb Elati's words belong to the chorus of men who must live in the world with order and rhythm. These are things men depend upon, the balance which makes life possible. Hovering over this order is the word of God. If the word must find a dwelling, it is man who gives it its place in the world. It finds its place in the commentaries. The fate of the rabbis is the commentary. In their words, we comprehend the fate of God's word in its dwelling. Where would the divine word be without the rabbis? They are its guardian, and through the generations, they have searched for its meaning. They have questioned its meaning and purposes, given answers which brought forth new questions. Their rhythm is in the

---

[17]Ibid.
[18]Ibid.

question and the answer. Like the rising and setting of the sun, the questions and answers flow from each other only to be repeated in new and novel forms. The music of their voices astounds us with its choruses of questions and answers. The tones and harmonies allow us to feel the divine presence. There is a singing which goes through humankind, rising and falling with interrogations. We listen to the sounds which emerge from man's longing to know the word of God. But it can only be heard in song, in that singsong movement of devotion and courage.

The commentaries among the rabbis are never finished. They are the never-ending dialogues between man and the word. They are the responses of the community to history and its responsibility. These commentaries bear witness to the absence of God. In his presence, there are no commentaries. "All letters give form to absence. Hence, God is the child of His Name."[19] The pen often denies the voice, the gesture, the tone, the rhythm which is alive in human conversation. We have to imagine these expressions of feeling. They flee from the written words and die on the whiteness of the page. We have only the signs that dwell in our words.

The divine words speak of God's absence. The presence of his words is the reality of his absence. Presence and absence are abstract terms. The poet gathers about them the endless paths of human life. The love story of Yukel and Sarah hovers around the commentaries and the dialogues. It reveals how deeply life has been wounded in our generation, perhaps more gravely wounded than in previous generations. Dialogues and commentaries are not enough to comprehend the depths of human suffering. The tragedy of inescapable suffering demands its very presence. Without it we lose the individual and the reality of his existence.

Reb Jobi said: "Wound me as you struck my forebears and my father. I can only feed on my humiliated blood."[20] We feed on more than the humiliated blood. From the book has come our purpose in the world, the reality of bearing witness to a God who is no longer with us, but who dominates our lives through his absence. We have remained faithful even in his absence. The wound that was inflicted upon us never heals. We are the people who dwell alone. The world rarely has a place for such a people. They are wounded wherever they dwell.

"One morning when we were lying on the beach, she traced her initials in the sand with her forefinger. S.S. Sarah Schwall. S.S.S.S. (What was his name, Sarah? The young SS officer who wore your initials engraved in his soul, who went everywhere thanks to your initials, who

---

[19]Ibid., 47.
[20]Ibid., 145.

wore a uniform designated by them?... He was not the only one to glory in the prestige of the double letter. There were millions to glory with him. How could you have resisted them inside your own name?"[21] The letters of Sarah's name are evaporating into the two letters of evil SS. We feel the goodness of Sarah Schwall fade away into an evil that is not only present for the moment, but is eternally present. In Sarah we face the dread of evil which we don't want to recognize; it is in us, has always found a dwelling among us. Sarah and Yukel bear the pain and madness which the people have borne and will bear struggling to be loyal to an absent God. Where lies the hope for this suffering if not in faith? Perhaps in the commentaries and dialogues which we write? The commentaries are the histories which we write again and again, forcing us to remember a history which we have made, and which has been made for us. Sarah and Yukel walk through a world which no longer belongs to them. They have been taken from the world by those who didn't want them to live with their God. We know biographically little of Sarah and Yukel. This makes it impossible for us to isolate and remove them from our memories. They are more than a particular incident. Sarah and Yukel wander the world which turns from them in embarrassment. Their voices belong to the silence which harbors the powers of evil. The silence of evil lies in the lie which speaks, through the signs which distort and the attitudes which corrupt.

Jabès begins "The Book of the Living" with these words: "When the yellow star was shining in the sky of the accursed, he wore the sky on his chest. The sky of youth with the wasp's sting, and the sky with the armband of mourning. He was seventeen. An age with wide margins."[22] The poetry which speaks of the yellow star and the armband gathers to it the voices of a world which has come near to its demise. Words which show us the reality of human existence force us to honor the word which brought forth the creation. The word is our precious gift. With it we struggle to comprehend what is always beyond our imagination, but leans upon it and causes us to wonder about things we don't comprehend, but only approach. Here lie the paradoxes, and the sources of our parables. We cannot suppress this longing to understand. We know that we will never master the understanding, but are always mastered by it. The deeper we wander into histories and commentaries, the more we realize that they are our substitutes for the facts which will never be ours, for the feelings and needs which have captured our meditations. The yellow star is a badge we can never remove. It is the badge we have been given by the generations. The badge is our reality,

---

[21]Ibid., 145-46.
[22]Ibid., 155.

the mark of identification. People recognize us with it. When we forget it, they return it to us. We wear it like an indelible possession. "When the yellow star was shining in the sky of the accursed, [we wore the sky on our] chest. From one night to the next, day is the hardest stage."[23] There is no other way to live if we discard the yellow badge. We fade into oblivion.

The story of Sarah and Yukel is that of the yellow badge of "a situation without grass, without leaves." The story of Sarah is the revelation of the yellow badge. Sarah's life unfolds through the commentaries and dialogues. She is the mother of the people. They were born from her and to her they return. Sarah is the eternal mother. She, at fourteen, "wanted to be a teacher. Instead of joining her classmates on holidays, she gathered children around her, whom she taught to use words (to let them be caught by them), whom she told stories of light and darkness. They listened as one might listen to the colors of the world monologuing until evening."[24] Sarah belonged to the children. In her words, she showed them the love of the mother, the power of familial relationship. In their words, the future was born. The children would carry with them the force of her words. These words would never leave them. Sarah and the children gave witness to the never-ending truth that "childhood is a colony of words which the years are set on dispersing." The sufferings of Sarah wear the label of the SS. They placed the yellow badge where it has been for the generations, the label given to Israel by those who deny its birthright. Sarah the mother, Abraham the father, brought forth a people that came from their union, a people of God. But it was this divine relation which brought forth the rancor of others. In it, Israel found its purpose and love, a witness to God in the world. Men sought other gods, and from Moloch to the SS, these gods found their children. They sent them to conquer and destroy the children of Sarah.

The poet evokes the name of Sarah to speak of her tears and her beauty:

> Sarah, Sarah, is this here the beginning of the world?
> We don't want to miss out on anything
> Is today the creation of the world? It is, isn't it?
> The world has been created. But wasn't it destroyed?
> Sarah, Sarah, what was the first thing in the world?
> The word? Looking? Tell us, what was first?
> What, Sarah? Do tell. The world is a whole.
> Is it round like the head? Round like a hoop? Just a circle?
> But the woods, Sarah? Yes, and school, Sarah?

---

[23]Ibid.
[24]Ibid., 155-56.

Yes, yes, and the sea and the mountains?[25]

The lines are read and heard. There is no message. There is no message to be proclaimed. The voices that are evoked in the poem speak four words: "My name is Sarah." In these words, we hear the voice of the creation, as in the words "I am who I am," we hear the words of God. In Sarah's words, the earth speaks. We hear of birth and children, of woods and seas, of shapes and sounds. We hear of the beautiful and the sublime, of love and tenderness, but there are also sounds of destruction and madness. Sarah Schwall becomes SS. The letters are drawn into the destruction of the name. Suddenly we are aware of the meaning of the name, of the Holy Name. The name can fade away, drawn into oblivion. Moloch, the name of evil, eats children, and Sarah struggles for their protection. Her heart gives birth to the love and sensitivity in which they are led from childhood to adulthood. Again and again we confront the struggle between Sarah and Moloch. Sarah gathers her children in devotion and goodness. She is the teacher whose standards are decency and probity. Sarah stands before her people, i.e., before the world as the embodiment of humaneness. But Sarah is always threatened. Her children have been destroyed. There is a covenant between her and God, but even this can be subverted and shattered. Samson R. Hirsch commented: "Accordingly, the same covenant that was made with Abraham earlier is now reiterated explicitly as applicable also to Sarah. [God said to Abraham]: Without her, I could never have made My covenant with you... *She* shall become nations: *her* character shall live on in tribes of the promised nation...."[26]

Sarah has seen the children of the earth devastated in body and soul, "hearts and brains which were nothing but a heap of rubble." Sarah looks with pain upon her children and is helpless before the powers of Moloch. Sarah has listened to history. She has witnessed the misery of man and the torture of children. Sarah, with courage and persistence, is love and tenderness. She is there telling us that the children must be saved, that in them are the hopes of humankind; in every society and community, the children are the measure of its worth and value. Sarah lives the covenant with God. She is the noble commandment of humankind: You shall educate, and not only instruct, your children. Sarah inherited from the biblical Sarah the stubbornness of her people. Sarah, like her namesake, burned with love. She faced the Moloch of the SS. Sarah now wore the yellow badge and would die for the love of mother Sarah with whom God made the covenant. Moloch never dies,

---

[25]Ibid., 156-57.
[26]S.R. Hirsch, *The Pentateuch,* trans. G. Hirschler (New York: Judaica Press, 1990), 85; commentary to Gen., 17:16.

but Sarah never surrenders her children without the scream that shakes and frightens humankind. Sarah's scream emerged from a faith which could not be quenched, which even afflicted God, which aroused the heavens and startled the angelic hierarchies. Sarah voiced the sufferings of her children. She sought their protection. She remembered the covenant. God was silent.

Sarah is the scream of motherhood. Sarah Schwall knows that she belongs to this scream, the piercing voice of mother Sarah which fills the world when her children are threatened and Moloch has again gained dominance in the world. Sarah's agony fills every soul that knows of the conversion of the children into creatures of the state, the disruption of the loyalties of the family, and, above all, the separation of mother from child, the violence and terror of Moloch. From Sarah's protection of the child, civilization is born. Sarah bears witness to the covenant, to the love of child and family. Never is this love more intense than before the god of child sacrifice, before Moloch. "The owl howling against the wind," asks Sarah, "is it me. Yukel, is it me? The owl against the wind, the owl for the wind? Is it me? Yukel, is it me? The wind sweeping off my screams, my screams exasperating the wind?"[27] Sarah's screams reveal her madness. They are the screams of desperation. God is absent. Sarah is alone. She can no longer protect her children. Moloch draws them unto himself. Sarah weeps.

"Sarah, Yukel, United kingdoms, innocent worlds, which the alphabet conquered and then destroyed through the hands of men. You have lost your kingdom. I have lost my kingdom, as my brothers have, scattered everywhere in a world which has feasted on their dispersion. Have you seen how a kingdom is made and unmade? Have you seen how a book is made and unmade?"[28] We remain in the world with questions which reveal how distant and irreconcilable the contradictions are from each other. They are so far from each other that they don't know each other. We pretend to bring them together to satisfy our curiosity. We have only our questions, and these reveal the wonders and madness which embrace the lives of the children of Abraham and Sarah. With the poet, we wander through history and seek to understand. We find only questions, the violence and terror of questions. With the poet, we walk slowly, but courageously. He bears with him the book and the desert. No matter where he is, they are with him. He teaches us to live with and from them. They talk to us of our destiny, of the hate that surrounds us, but also of the covenant with Abraham and Sarah, of the source of

---

[27]*The Book of Questions*, 167.
[28]Ibid., 175.

beauty, of goodness and holiness. "All beginnings are invisible, we learn to see little by little. In this way, the book is made [Yukel's Notebook]."[29]

We have a companionship with the poet and we must travel further with him. We don't understand the beginning(s), but it conditions the travels we make. We don't comprehend the poet. We want to talk with him further. Yukel came back from the ashes. We needed to speak with him. There are questions we must ask. Answers must be pierced.

---

[29]Ibid., vol. II:16.

5

The Presence and Absence
of Yukel and Sarah

"In the cemetery of Bagneux, *département de la Seine,* rests my mother. In old Cairo, in the cemetery of sand, my father. In Milano, in the dead marble city, my sister is buried. In Rome, where the dark dug out the ground to receive him, my brother lies. Four graves. Three countries. Does death know borders? One family. Two continents. Four cities. Three flags, one language: of nothingness. One pain. Four glances in one. Four lives. One scream. Four times, a hundred times, a thousand times one scream. And those who were not buried? asked Reb Azel. And all the shadows in the world are screams, replied Yukel."[1]

Who, we ask, can comprehend and feel these words? Experience demands experience. Words float above experience and are lost in the mist, but others rise from and fall into it. These are the words of the exiles who in their adopted lands remain exiles, who in the land of Israel believe they have ended their exile. But Israel will always be an exile, the child of Sarah and Abraham. Dwelling alone is the destiny of this people who must always dwell with others. Only with them does Israel understand and experience what it means to dwell alone. Sarah's children are buried in the soil of the world. They have traveled to all peoples in search of peace, and freedom from persecution. The poet leads us from exile to exile, through the lands of commentaries and dialogues. From the piercing voices of the past the people hear of their greatness and their suffering. They are a productive and creative people, giving their neighbors works of art and science. They know the vanity of the world, but also the wonders that lie in it.

---

[1]*The Book of Questions,* vol. 3, 145.

Will the world cease hearing Sarah's screams? is a question we need to pose again and again. What would the world be without the voice of Sarah? It would lose its spiritual quality. We would no longer dream of the future in which the rupture between matter and form would narrow, in which God's absence would illume his presence, in which Sarah's goodness would dominate Moloch, and children would not only be instructed, but also educated. Forgetfulness diminishes the moral quality of human existence, but remembrance enhances and deepens the moral integrity of human life. We are forced again and again to value and revalue the meaning of forgetfulness and remembrance in the commentaries we make. We must talk about our existence. We need to inquire into the purpose of life, the meaning of history, and the dreams of the future. The prophet Joel told us of these dreams: "I will pour out my spirit in all flesh; your sons and daughters shall prophesy; your old men shall dream dreams. And your young men shall see visions. I will even pour out my spirit upon male and female slaves in those days" (Joel 3:1-2). We hear much from all these directions. We travel on many paths. Hope joins despair, the past joins the future, while the dream emerges from dreams and the vision from the vision.

Wherever the poet leads us, we attempt to follow, but we travel with experience. We have learned to listen and see. We read the poet, but always in dialogue with the poetry of our soul, with the visions and dreams that have been our paths. We follow the poet to enhance our being, to verify and discover its depths and limitations. We are fructified by the experiences which fill our reality. We long for contradiction and challenge.

"God died with my childhood," wrote Reb Guebra. "He died with my youth. Now he is dying with me. In the eternal void, three fiery arrows thus recall a man's passing, perhaps his last question? And Yukel said: Was Reb Guebra a good or bad rabbi?... Did he, like those inspired men who were condemned for their bold ideas, commit the sacrilege of challenging the Law of God? If so, he no doubt deserved that people turn from him. And from me too, for of all the rabbis who have their place in the book, Reb Guebra is most like me."[2]

Much is said by the poet about the dying of God. What he says intrigues us because each of us knows that God dies, each of us knows that the God of our youth must die, as every moment of God is a dying in us. Would there be a God if he didn't die? We find it difficult to struggle with God, to wrench from him a moment of actuality. We hear from psalmists and saints a repetition of these bitter words: "How long, O Lord, will you ignore me forever? How long will you hide your face

---

[2]Ibid., 147.

from me? How long will I have cares on my mind, grief in my heart all day? How long will my enemy have the upper hand?" (Ps. 13:2-4). The words *how long* never leave us. God is always with us, but never is he there as a possession. He is there so that His presence makes us aware of his absence, so that we discover the nature of our mortality. The dying of God is the venture of the living God. His silence is his voice, his love is his hiddenness, his unfathomable Being is always beyond itself. Jabès's God is beyond the being captured by the faiths of religions. He is the formless reality of forms which Jabès experienced in the desert outside of Cairo. In the speechless speech and the formless forms, Jabès found hints of God. He knew that only poetry could reveal God.

Reb Salinas said: "Our first breath comes from the most remote past; our last still owes it its warmth."[3] We are bound to a past from which there is no liberation. This binding, which is forever mirrored in Isaac, has no parallel to the deification of national traditions, to original tribal forms, and to racial purities. This binding belongs to the divine covenant. We stand covenanted to no earthly tradition, to no romantic past. The covenant of Noah is with God, a covenant both for Israel and mankind. The binding determined a divine-human relationship from which followed a human relationship. In rupture we discover madness and death. For every man there is a binding to either a contract or to a covenant. Human life discovers its beginnings in the binding. We listen to the words of the book and we hear: "I will maintain My covenant with you: never again shall all flesh be cut off by the waters of a flood, and never again shall there be a flood to destroy the earth.... I have set My bow in the clouds, and it shall serve as a sign of the covenant between Me and the earth (Gen. 9:11-12).

We wander from value to value, from profession to communal activity, from tradition to reason, and we remain with unsatisfying answers to the meaning and purpose of life. Beyond our earthly journeys are the divine beginnings, the timeless figures of Noah, Sarah, Abraham, Isaac, and Jacob. These are the startling dialogues which prepare the foundations of humankind, but even more deeply the paths which men will follow in the generations to come. The beginnings create the end. Journeys are always circular. We will always hear the command to Abram to go forth from his native land, the blessing given to Sarah: "I will bless her so that she shall give rise to nations; rulers of people shall issue from her" (Gen. 17:16). Visions and dreams fill our souls as we remember the words of the beginnings, the images they created and the intense intimacy they evoked between man and man. We have only our

---

[3]Ibid., 151.

separations and ruptures. They reveal our reality. We are men of rupture and commentary.

Jabès spoke to us in meditative tones at the beginning of the third *Book of Questions*, which he called *Return to the Book*. "It is years," he said, "since I left Egypt. A succession of landings mark the repose of centuries, of death. Truth is not for sale. We are our own truth: this is the solitude of God and man. It is our common freedom. Hail to the only, the universal Truth. We try to reach it by innumerable roads whose indirection we are. Truth is in the movement toward it. It is also in the coming of a counter-truth wrapped in mystery.... In the desert no thought takes the lead, no dream."[4] We separate truths from each other. There is the primordial moment in which truths fade into each other, into truth itself. In this moment, there is only truth, the abyss in which there is no measure and form. The desert is the formlessness of forms, the soundless reality of sounds. The tones and rhythms of the desert defy our search for definitions, but it is into this world without definitions that each of us must journey, and journey again and again. Here we are cleansed of the forms we have assumed, of the formulas we habitually acquire, of the fixities and oddities we called life. The desert is the purification which is demanded of us by the concreteness of our travels. The way to and away from the desert is the turn and return toward the truth that is no longer possible for us in the world of necessity, governed by the inescapable laws of power and self-deification. But the return to the desert, to spiritual purification, is the beginning from which everything begins. The desert makes it possible for us to hear the word, to hear what must be heard above the din of everyday life, above the particularities of the arts and the sciences. We search to regain the presence of the word. In the absence it is the word which is still speaking. We seek to recover the speaking word.

"I have followed a book in its persistence, a book which is the story of a thousand stories as night and day are the prow of a thousand poems. I have followed it where day succeeds the night and night the day, where the seasons are four times two hundred and fifty seasons."[5] The poet told us that he followed the book. Nothing else seems to have meaning for him. The book is the book of life. Every human creation is written in the book; it is a commentary to the book. Man, like a painting, a scientific theory, a poem, or a novel, is a child of the book. Some of the children we call antique, others modern, some appeal to us, some are indifferent, but in them all we find the word of the book, the creative word, which men have used in various and distinct ways. The book has the word of God. It

---

[4]Ibid., 153.
[5]Ibid., 159.

is voiced in the word of man. We know of the difference between them. They belong together, dependent upon each other. The word is in exile, gathering the words of the beginning, the words that were God's, and now are alone in exile longing to be redeemed by man. Man redeems these words through the reason, and goodness, that is in him. Man's redemptive work is revealed in the spirit, in the never-ending attempt to embody the word in the creative act, in drama and vision, in action and theory. Man's modernity is the living spirit of the past. Man writes, paints, sculptures, in search of the powers of the spirit. Nothing is past, present, or future. Everything is embodied in the book. We are forever discovering it in what we see and write. Man is a unique discoverer. His life is formed in the unknown and unexpected. In the midst of the creation, man shows us the word of the discoverer.

"I am a man's wanderings, path and road. Had I so totally forgotten it? Calmly, resigned, and with manly consciousness, I accept the conditions laid down: to wander through reality and the dream of reality for which every syllable of the book is a reason."[6] Wandering is an adventure. It is a refusal to be resigned to a particular place and time. Each place and time is both a reality and the beginning of a different possibility. The poet searches for a wandering that is creativity. Wandering brings forth the other, what has not yet been seen and heard. Wandering is not an escape from the present. It is the search for the presence that dwells in the now. Man wanders through the present like the explorer of a new land, a new idea, a new relationship. Man wanders the earth to discover himself, to find the word which describes his movements, his unquenchable curiosity, the meaning and purpose of what he sees and hears both from the past and in the present. The wanderer refuses to bury the vision in a land, a religion, or in a tradition. For his personal existence he has accepted a tradition, a particular way of life. He defies this tradition by wandering inquisitively toward other forms and practices, whose ways he seeks to comprehend.

The wanderer knows that the world is changing. He is not aware of much that is going on about him. The present for him is a vast potential of knowledge and feelings, and he knows that its vastness has escaped him. Not only has much failed to become his reality. The reality which comes to him is beyond his control. He is like a speck of sand in the labyrinth of nothingness which is human life. He is a living and creative being who wanders because he is eager to know, to feel, and to dream. He is not overcome by ideology, restricted by nationalism, and tied by a particular history. He is a wanderer from a small tribe whose ancestors have lived in the lands of the earth, shared traditions, cultivated the arts

---

[6]Ibid., 162.

and sciences. Not only have they lived and shared with others, they have written commentaries, mystical contemplations, and have sought in visions the land of their forefathers. Their visions embraced a spiritual humanity, an idea of justice and humility. The enduring loyalty has been to their God whose law they preserve and whose word they attempt to embody in their texts. Wandering has been their life, but in and through it they have shown a distinct freedom of inquiry and speculation. The solitude of Israel is a unique spiritual and physical reality.

"Repetition," Jabès remarked, "is man's power to perpetuate himself in God's supreme speculations. To repeat the divine act in its First Cause. Thus man is God's equal in his power to choose an unpredictable Word which he alone can launch. I obey slavishly. I am master of the metamorphoses. Adventure is a property of words."[7] Wandering is not only movement; it is the creation of the word, the capacity to give form, tone, and rhythm to what is seen and heard. Wandering challenges the imagination. Man is an image maker. In this activity, he creates the world. Through his images he approaches God and embraces the divine act. The human adventure is more than tales of events and deeds; it challenges us to build descriptions, create metamorphoses, and explore parables and paradoxes. The wonder of the *Iliad* and the *Odyssey* are not only the events they describe, but the telling of them. The divine lies in the word. Jabès always spoke of wandering. He spoke of the wandering of the word, the challenge of it, the rupture between the word and the event. Wandering is the odyssey of freedom. The demise of man begins when he no longer dares to wander. Like man, the book also wanders; like the book, God wanders.

We listen to this song:

> By the wayside leaves
> So tired of being leaves
>   they fell
> By the wayside Jews
> So tired of being Jews
>   they fell
> Sweep up the leaves
> Sweep up the Jews
> Will the same leaves regrow in spring?
> Is there a spring for trampled Jews?[8]

We read the poem in the midst of our thoughts about the wanderings of the book. We experience the intimate relationship between prose and verse.

---

[7]Ibid., 162-63.
[8]Ibid., 166.

From one to the other, the commentaries continue like the wanderings of the man who knows that there is no end to his search for what is presence in the present. But man tires of his wandering. The tribe surrenders its devotion to the God of the desert, whose presence is now absence. The presences are now different. The absence of God has left them to man's endeavors, to his prose and his poetry, his endless search for their meaning, for the now which bears in it the unknown and unexpected. The latter are essential elements of the known and the expected. Man seeks to know what can be known, what lies beyond. The struggle for reality lies in that intimate dialogue between one and the other. Man is primarily a speaking being. Discourse is his way in the world. In discourse he finds the source of his interpretations.

"First I thought I was a writer. Then I realized I was a Jew. Then I no longer distinguished the writer in me from the Jew because one and the other are only torments of an ancient world."[9] We flee often from what binds us. We forget our ancestor Isaac, the binding which tied him to God and caused a rivalry between the bound and unbound that has continued through the generations. When we fled the divine, we sought him in new lands, in reason, in philosophies called Stoicism, Epicureanism, liberalism. When we flee a divine binding, we find a secular one. We exchange one bondage for another. But our God doesn't go away. He is there in silence and absence. Men are creatures of their traditions and faiths. In them, they have found their doubts and sufferings, and they long to go elsewhere, to other faiths and loves. In defiance of the divine, men search for the powers of rivalry and defiance. From the earliest times, men have sought to make God their partner, to restrict him to their words, and to control him in their actions. Again and again man has sought to explain his own ways, to reveal how dependent he is upon the tradition he has created from his devotion to God. Nothing is understandable for him unless he grasps the binding of a people to their God. In every thing we do, we bring the past into the present. We speak of the old and cause it to live in the now. The ancient names become modern, and suddenly we realize that our dialogues with our God are an attempt to give him presence. We do this either in defiance of him or in devotion to him.

Jabès filled our world with imagery. We realize that we have lost the immediate world of faces, feelings, and actions. Individuals come and go like fleeting figures. We hear of them through lines of speech, notebooks, and memories. Everything has been metamorphosed. Things point to one another. We discover the wonders of our imagination, and we ask whether it is not in this world of metaphors, images, and symbols that

---

[9]Ibid., 195.

truth is more apparent than in the concreteness which we have always assumed to be the real and the actual. It is not what we see, hear, or touch that is our essential reality, but rather the transformation, transfiguration, and translation of this material into visions and dreams. Whatever definitions we prefer to give to ourselves, we cannot escape the *fact* that we are the transformers of our reality. In our spirit, everything is changed either by the marvel of our hands or the creative powers of the mind. Everything we touch or see is transfigured, everything becomes a source of imaginative possibilities. The poet is precious to us. He shows us the way to these transformations. He teaches us the powers of judgment. He shows us the meaning and formation of ideas. In his words, we find that undetermined thought that is so powerfully rich with images and contingencies. These are the formative products which allow us to go forward and change the concrete into the spiritual. Here we touch the divine, putting forth our finger toward God's and realizing how close we are to him in the action of creation. Men can hear the words of the poet, but their meaning depends upon experience. Man's defiance of both spiritual and physical captivity is his greatness. Longing to imitate the divine, man has found his place between the divine and the animals.

Man's place in the universe is undefinable. Man remains animal as deeply as he remains spirit. Jabès remarked that "a tree introduces the woods. Among the dense trunks, climbing on branches, retracing his steps to start out in a new direction. The child follows an unchartered, dangerous path which his imagination sets free."[10] For the tree, the direction of growth is determined by soil and sun. Man lives with innumerable possibilities, many of which remain unknown and unexpected. Man remains forever unknown to himself. Man is the child of the question. He is uncomfortable with the answers. Answers close down possibilities. It is difficult for man to subdue the child within him. He longs to preserve the enthusiasm and love of discovery which are the essence of the child. Man knows that the child must be limited, but never eliminated. The child is the never-ending source of questions. He refuses to be the captive of the answer. "Word of fruit rather than roots. Word of sap and dew. The question has the soft colors of peaks rounded by dawn."[11] We suffocate the question to remain in peace with the answer. We tire of the question to find the captivity of the answer. Poetry awakens the child within us. We turn away from this child when we surrender the question to the answer. Man's life belongs to the joy which comes from the need for the question, from the unquenchable excitement

---

[10]Ibid., 196.
[11]Ibid., 197.

of discovery and the insatiable wonder which is awakened in us by the untraveled and unexperienced.

The man who never leaves the child surrenders the fruit to the source; the child who never leaves the man surrenders the source to the fruit. Neither one can be had without the other. The source is the enthusiasm of love; the fruit, its embodiment in form. We find it difficult to separate love from form. There can only be a loving knowledge, questions which prick our imagination, startle the mind, and soften our feelings. The mind needs the pleasures of the flesh, the finesse of the sensitivities, and the excitement of the adventure. The child and the man live and work together. They are harness and liberation. The child cannot leave the man. The man cannot leave the child.

We think of Abraham taking his son to the land of Moriah. The account tells us little of the conversation between the father and son. We have only one conversation. Isaac speaks to his father: "Father, and he answered, Yes my son, and he said, Here are the firestone and the wood, but where is the sheep for the burnt offering? And Abraham said, God will see to the sheep for His burnt offering, my boy. And the two of them walked in together" (Gen. 22:7-8). Here the conversation is constructed to show the depths of trust between father and son, a trust which lies in the relationship of faith. In its rupture, father and son lose their bonds. But trust is not enough. It can never destroy the question which must be both in father and in son. To be a man of faith is to question, to be a father is to have the trust of the son, but can that trust be without the question, without doubt? Neither the father nor the son can be without doubt. Faith, trust, and doubt form the intricate and intimate dialectic between man and man, and between God and man. The poet spoke of the question which is always with us, of the answers that are always shattered. We cannot imagine the three-day journey of the Moriah in silence. We imagine doubts, fears, questioning, but we think also of courage, devotion, and love. These opposites are alive in each other. They weave a human fabric of relationship which shows how deeply opposites depend upon each other.

Reb Assim remarked: "Interpreting the law is our daily task. Questioning the pledge of truth in God."[12] Jabès created a poetry of commentary and dialogue. He has formed discourses and discussions. Men are always speaking. They are not seeking speculative and theoretical systems or vast plans of comprehension. Jabès knew that there is no comprehension, no meaningful speculative system which commands human life. Such systems belong to the fanciful artistry of those who are convinced that their intellectual games create reality, that

---

[12]Ibid., 198.

their categories capture the intricacies of human thought, that the divine creative act has become part of the human experience. Jabès formed attitudes, explored feelings, and delicately balanced the need to know with the poetry of the unknown. We read with Jabès a world of images and meditations, and we are led to create others. With Jabès, thinking accompanies thinking. The poet creates in us the desire for adventure, but never do we know the outcome. Do we walk like Isaac in trust and devotion, do we claim to be "knights of faith" walking quietly and courageously toward the object of God's will, questioning nothing, but living from our own volition and trust? Hardly! Abraham is not the model. We are closer to the doubts and the questioner. His strength is strange to us. We feel intimate with those in whom there is "fear and trembling." They are the children of men rather than the children of God. In their fears and doubts, we find the discourses of humankind, the poetry of man's adventures with the divine absence. It is not the Patriarch who inspires us, but the screams of Sarah who is suffering for her children. We must imagine Abraham suffering. Only then can we call him the Father of the people.

"The book is a labyrinth. You think you are leaving and only get in deeper. You have no chance of running off. For that, you must destroy the work. You cannot make up your mind to do that. I notice your anxiety mounting. Slowly but surely. Wall after wall. Who awaits you at the end? Nobody. Who will leaf through you, decipher, love you? No doubt, nobody. You are alone in the night, alone in the world.... Alas. Nobody ventures here. The book bears your name. Your name clenched like a fist, clenched in a sword."[13]

Man's life in the world is a dialogue which he discovers and attempts to pursue. For the Jew, it is the dialogue with the book, the unending commentaries he writes. He seeks to find the meaning of the book. But the book is greater than its commentaries. It is greater than the faith of men. Again and again, man attempts to relate to the book, but he must choose within its vastness what is possible for him. The book allows man to see how small is life, how overwhelming is God. Man asks himself repeatedly how firm is his devotion and trust. Man is alone in the world with the book. The book reveals the rupture between the divine and the human. Man cannot overcome this rupture. He lives the reality of it. He lives in its solitude. Man has no way to pierce the wall. Walls lead to walls. On every wall our fate is written. We are captives of a book from which there is no escape, a book which has created us, which we love in suffering. There is no escape from the confrontation with the book, no shirking the courage and endurance which it demands

---

[13]Ibid., 201.

of us. The people who have been not only instructed, but educated, by the book have been given the gift of endurance. They have brought this endurance to every aspect of life, to the arts and sciences, to literature and politics. The people learn the meaning of the absence of God. The forces of necessity dominate their lives.

Reb Kahn remarked: "You do not see the Name, but you read it. Is the invisible not also unreadable? I write. I see the Name you read."[14] The invisible is both readable and unreadable. Readable as we write and give it form, yet the form we give it becomes unreadable and formless. We find a strange and enchanting movement between the readable and invisible. We adventure into the realm of images, seeking to bring the invisible into the visible through images, parables, metaphors. We succeed in our writing. We believe we have manipulated the word and forced it to reveal a moment of the invisible, allowing us to think of that harmony between spirit and matter which men have longed for in their poems to God.

In every man lives a modicum of theosophy. We read the Holy Name and we feel that it has become ours, a precious and sacred possession, but the Holy Name is not a possession. It is the radical other, the transcendent we long for with love, a love which finds no consummation but which must reach out beyond itself. The Holy Name pierces our finite actions. We speak of it, and we find it but its reality written in the texts, both encourages and defies our images and dreams. In the defiance, the reality grows in intensity. We love the divine profoundly because we cannot have nor dominate it. What we control, we despise. The invisible is our true love. We discover it in a person, in an idea whose reality we cannot control, in the divine who is the light of our light.

"One night in the desert," wrote Reb Adeba, "while scrutinizing the sky for an answer to my love, I saw a star disappear and, as if breaking with an eternal order, melt into another star whose sudden brightness I could not but admire. Was I a victim of my own imagination? Soon after, the star reappeared. Then I told myself that I had followed the track of its innermost desire and that my dazzled eyes had for a moment made possible the alliance of two stars."[15] In search of an answer a star disappeared, and we wonder if there could be some relationship between the search and the disappearance of the star. The star merged with another and their brightness startled me. We wondered if we had imagined this or if our sight had shown us a verifiable occurrence. How could we judge between the one and the other? We realized that life

---

[14]Ibid., 205.
[15]Ibid., 216.

gives us no measure between imagination and verification and, if it did, the circumstances would be controlled and limited. If one related to the other, then the realities of human life would move between the demands of verification and the claims of the imagination. We cannot unite them. They come close to each other, but separate easily from each other. They seem to attract and repulse each other. My eyes bring them together. What other reality could be called and not found lacking? There are no facts, no objective truths, no verifiable data; what you see in the sky is a figment, an illusion, a chimera. The latter are the creations of arbitrariness and dream. They are not the work of a true science, of a soul enlivened only by the truth of experimentation. The imagination is exiled in such surroundings and becomes an alien reality. But someone may ask if the deification of objectivity doesn't lie in its own imaginative powers, its own capacity to create with the poetic insight, to look beyond its data and create with dreams and visions, to realize that qualitative facts are inadequate and hardly absolute. The fact is open to a world that surpasses it, that comes to it from above. With our eyes, we look up. We bring to what we have achieved what has not yet approached us from the unknown.

Jabès's poetry moves in delicate curves from the present to the beginnings. We feel the circular movement of thought drawing from the beginnings what the present is continually making manifest. The deepening and expanding powers of the mind make it possible to be inspired and moved by the past. Reflections and meditations return again and again to the same realities, but always differently. There is no assurance that what has been said will be surpassed by what is being said. There is no linear progress. There are changes in attitudes and perspectives. There is a subtle dialectic by which thought comes into contact with thought. The contact is unpredictable, and what arises from it remains inadequate. Everywhere the unknown and the unexpected appear, but they move together with themes which remain constant. We read the text differently each day. The fluidity of the poet's prose and verse make it impossible to repeat what we have previously grasped. We move along, conscious only of the vastness of thought which the poet puts before us, knowing that each time we have the text it becomes an adventure, which we can limit but not control.

"God gives Himself to God. He refuses Himself to man. Thus God's eternity is in refusal, said Reb Amra. Does man give himself to man in the love of God? Not in love, Reb Amra went on, but in His dazzling Absence. Alone in the morning, God sees. Is man on his way toward man within the divine eyes? Adonai contemplates Adonai. Man moves with the eye of God fixed on His own image."[16]

We speak again and again of God's absence and we understand it as little as we understand the reality of God's presence. The words confound us. We are alone with them knowing neither their meaning nor their purpose, but we are bound to God and seek to be named in the book. We cannot endure the solitude of God even when we search for it within ourselves. We need to be named by the Holy Name. But there is truth in his absence as there is truth in his presence. There is no separation between his absence and his presence. They are one. Absence makes it possible to dream of him, to struggle with images and visions of his presence. God's absence makes it possible for us to be men, to find within ourselves the powers of creativity, what we call the dignity of man. Man must call to man, must turn himself toward the other, toward the sovereignty that lies in his reason. This turning is necessary because God contemplates only himself, is absorbed in his word. Man is set free by the presence of the word to find within himself the powers from which emerge the arts and sciences. This liberation is continuous. It takes place with the divine-human relationship. The turning of man toward himself and the other is not a victory over the divine, but the realization that man's movements depend upon the divine. We turn from God to find man. It is the presence of God that makes it possible for man to search for those powers which lie within himself. They are the powers of dependence. We cry in love for divine recognition, but in this cry we search for the autonomy which gives us our dignity.

Concluding the *Return to the Book*, Jabès noted his attitude in this adventure from the desert to the book and from the book to the desert. He said: "Book rejected and reclaimed by the book. The word, for which I was pain and meditation, discovers that its true place is the non-place where God lives resplendent with not being, with never having been. Therefore, interpretations of Elohim, approaches to Adonai, can only be personal, laws only individual laws, truths only solitary truths in the screams they wrench from us. And this even within the possibility of transmitting a recognized Truth, a common and sealed law."[17]

As we move through the great circles of thought, interrupted and begun anew, perfect in thought, imperfect in actuality, we realize how wondrously our thinking takes us from one level of thinking to another, how it moves from subjectivity to objectivity, from presence to absence, from forms to chaos, from violence to order. We cannot escape the personal, the realization that we create the forms and images in which

---

[16]Ibid., 228.
[17]Ibid., 232.

the reality about us becomes meaningful and purposeful. Nothing exists without our interpretation. We mold and paint, sculpture and construct, what we perceive. We live with the splendors and miseries of our constructions, with our moral courage and weakness. Before us live Sarah and Yukel, and as we write our commentaries we think of the rooms in which they lived, of the pain and madness they suffered. We cannot escape our thinking; it accompanies us like our remembrances, those which the poet embraced, and those which dwell in us. Yukel said: "This is the room. The bed, the table, the walls, the roof. Here lived Sarah. Here lived Yukel. There is as much reality in these two rooms, these two dwellings, as in the street, the camps, the clinic where Sarah was taken. "In the book reality learns and reveals what it is: a visible irreality which we confront with itself, with the base in the summoned word."[18]

Does God exist? Does man exist? All we know is that Yukel and Sarah exist through the world, like the book exists through God and man. Things exist only through each other, through the mystery of relationships. All around we discover these relationships and search to find their meanings. We find only a circular movement which draws us back to the beginnings, to resemblances, to the desert, to the book, and the absence of God. As we finish one adventure with Jabès, we are prepared for the next. Ends become beginnings as beginnings come to ends.

---

[18]Ibid., 235.

6

A Conversation among the Scholars:
A Nondialogic Dialogue

In Yukel's notebook there is the following entry: "Faced with the impossibility of writing, which paralyzes every writer, and the impossibility of being Jewish, which has for two thousand years racked the people of that name, the writer chooses to write, and the Jew to survive."[1] One day, one week, one year, we don't know when, but there is a time, a place, and we are suddenly aware that our freedom has been captured by destiny. We cannot decide not to write; we must write. We don't have the ability to escape being a Jew; we hide from it, we become absorbed in humankind, we turn from religion, but it is in vain. Writing has made us a writer; the world has made us a Jew. At what point this has happened is of little consequence, but that it has occurred is of supreme importance. We are suddenly aware that there is a relationship between freedom and destiny that is beyond definition, which defies our capacity to isolate and confine. We believe that there is a bridge between one and the other, but even the bridge fades away. Left with this reality, we confront it graciously or retreat in disappointment. The journey has begun. Where it leads, we have no idea. It is a journey of destiny, and we are driven like the poets from land to land, traveling to places we don't know. Freedom dissolves into fate and fate assumes the air of freedom. We choose what has chosen us. We choose the chosen. We are no longer free beings living from choice to choice. We understand a new reality, one in which freedom is announced as destiny, and destiny is our free choice. "God is leaning against the dismantled wall of the Temple. From now on, no leveling will be ours – Reb Lahan."[2]

---

[1]*The Book of Questions*, 3:55.
[2]Ibid., 65.

We enter into a conversation between scholars and chance guests. Yukel takes part. If we listen to the scholars, and the others, we might have something to say. We don't want to merely record the conversation. We listen, but we would like to talk. Before we listen to the conversation, we should cite another entry from Yukel's notebook: "Difficulty of becoming part of the word and sharing its fate. Difficulty of bearing a Jewish soul and body. I write because while trying to get to the end of what I could say, I think every time, that the next time will succeed. God is silent for having once spoken in God's language."[3] Speaking, like writing, reflects our search for the meaning of our relationship to the word, to bearing its messages, to being part of the history in which the word was hidden and spoken in paradoxes and parables. The word was always there. The few bore it in their souls and felt its burden. Often they sought to shake it off and become like other people. But the word never let them go. They remain the people of the book, the people who question, those who confront their God without intermediaries and who live with the words of Balaam: "There is a people that dwells apart, not reckoned among the nations" (Num. 23:9). The solitude of the people accompanies the rupture that lives from the silence of God. This silence speaks of God's domination. Through silence God opens the reality of the word of man, the conversations which are necessitated by it, and which come to life through it. In the presence of "God's language" the human voice falls into abysmal quietude, human action becomes mechanical, and man dies. Man's hopes are nurtured in the divine absence. In this absence there is commentary and conversation.

The conversation among the scholars begins with these remarks: "I settle down in my work, but the work is unaware of it. The more I care about what I write, the more I cut myself off from the sources of my writing. The more sincere I want to be, the faster the words take over. I cannot refuse to let them exist without me."[4] The first scholar reminds us of how personal is the relationship between the writer and his words. More often we feel that our words are our instruments, to be used and forgotten. But the words become our companions. They come forth again and again to help us express the thoughts that are important to us. We find no comfort in the battle between the mind and the word. There is no victory for one over the other. Each is an essential part of the other. The word is the cloth on which I express my ideas. I feel the need to have the words serve the purpose of my thoughts. I cultivate them, and the order in which I place them. They are there haphazardly for me to use, but their use demands finesse and care. I hear them speak, I listen to the

---

[3]Ibid., 56.
[4]Ibid., 56.

intonation and rhythm they make. The words are not just vocables; they are cultivated forms which I again and again move about giving them order. The order reveals hints of beauty. I am pleased with the sounds and the precision. My thoughts take on the appearance I always wanted for them. Slowly there is a symmetry between my ideas and my expressions. My mind was inadequate without the words, and the words have no life without the mind. I think and I write and there is great pleasure in their harmony.

The first scholar continues: "And yet I am at the origin of their existence. I am, therefore, the man who conceived the verbal being which will have a fate of its own on which, in turn, my fate as a writer depends."[5] There can be no doubt that I am the source of my writing. I am the source of its fate and it is the source of mine. We realize this relationship with excitement and sadness. The word allows me to feel the creativity that is analogous to the divine. I know that my mortality is touched by the immortal, and that I am deeply dependent upon this relationship. The fate of my existence is determined in it. But there is the idea of humankind, a sensitivity for man's creative desires, an awareness of how dependent we are upon the freedom to think and act. The knowledge that we share this with our fellow beings, that we are a community and belong to each man, cuts through the exaggeration of individuality and brings us closer to community. If I am a writer, then it is the bond between the word and the thought which is vital to my existence. The word is precious, and must be defended against jargon which became the trademark of ideologies. On a lesser realm the protection of the word is vital. We protect it in conversation, in lectures, conferences, and on paper. The writer is the protector of the word that has become his property. In fact, the writer's relationship to the word is similar to that of his relationship to the book. We have wandered through the universe guided by the book; we have lived from its inspiration and seen its texts change and move in many directions. We have protected the legitimacy of these paths, although we have traveled only on one. The book can never become our property to be singularly interpreted and revealed. We have loved the invisible because it is invisible and we have loved the book because it is the book. The writer loves the power he cannot capture or control. He loves what he must pursue, what he longs for and can only approach. He loves the fate that has given him the undetermined thought.

"One morning," wrote Reb Assad, "sitting up in bed, I noticed that I have overnight been sawed apart from top to bottom. Ever since I have

---

[5]Ibid.

vainly tried to save both halves of myself."[6] This tale of Reb Assad broke
into the conversations among the scholars for no particular reason. I
thought it should be here. Every discussion has many levels, and every
participant brings to it part of his existence. In speaking, the particular
voice comes forth attempting to discover how to maintain a harmony
which never existed, and which if it did would reduce man to silence.
Knowing that life could never be harmonious, except in madness and
passivity, man, nevertheless, tries to find bridges between the halves
which will always remain apart from each other.

Another scholar stated: "I write and right away I become the word
which escapes me and thanks to which I am the word which leads to
other words and asserts itself as such. I am multiplied in my sentence as
a tree unfolds in its branches."[7] I write and I expand the possibilities of
my creative powers. If, like the tree, I emerge with branches in all
directions, then I am aware that some will be strong, others weak, some
long and others short, some will die, others will yield new branches,
some will shade the ground, others leave their leaves to the winds.
Where, I think, does my strength lie? Am I the branches which are like
lifted arms, moving toward the Creator, or am I the cover of the earth?
We know little of ourselves, but there is the choice from which none of us
escapes. I cannot be all the branches moving with different motions
because, unlike the tree, I don't nourish them naturally nor do I want to.
I live with preferences and in these I give precedence to one over the
other.

A third scholar joined and said: "An unformulated thought means
hope to join word to word, means waiting for signs in search of their
graven form, means possibility of unquestioned power to assent to
misery."[8] The unformulated thought is not a misfortune, but a richness
yet to be realized and comprehended. We have not yet found the correct
order of the words. We are aware that we may never find such an order.
Thought has powers which no order can confine and limit. There is the
"possibility of the unquestioned power" which reveals the quality of
man's mortality. We are displeased when we must confront a power
which we can contemplate but cannot define. In fact, we cannot place it
among our storehouse of clichés and lapidary sayings which seem to
have a place in varied situations. The confrontation with a spiritual
power which causes in us a feeling of awe is the source of the
imagination and the dream. We realize that the world doesn't fit into our
words; there are realities which remain "unclear ideas," and it is from

---

[6]Ibid., 15.
[7]Ibid., 56.
[8]Ibid.

this uncertainty that we draw strength and images. The third scholar brought us close to a reality that touches the imagination, nourishes it, but refuses to be limited by it.

The fourth scholar spoke like his colleagues: "I enter the neatly sectioned world of the alphabet with the few letters which recall me. What a distance between the will to be and the wording of this will, between perception and its spontaneous communication confirmed by the word. What I am is only what I will be without me."[9] We feel the contradictions that permeate existence and we believe we understand them, not only because we experience them, but because we realize that they are an essential part of our humanity. Reading the words of this scholar suddenly drew me to that enchanting work of Diderot, *D'Alembert's Dream*, where we feel and hear the contrary moods of the varied human paths. Grasping the difference between the I Am and the Me, the force that goes outward and the one that goes inward, I am conscious that they are the one and the many at the same time. I cannot know the one without knowing the other. If I can comprehend both on their legitimate paths, then I am close to the center of movements which give insights into their dependence. But I am rarely close to this center. I am always between what I am and what I will to be, what I write and what I desire to write. I am presence and absence.

Then another scholar said: "We do not know beforehand what regions we will cross because the end is between the tracks of adventures, between the lines, never between standing columns."[10] The tracks are fixed projections, they are aimed at a singular point, but life has no such point. It lies between the tracks, in the no-man's-land of the undefined, the ambiguous, and the unknown. Life is always in between the lines of the impossible, the changeless, and the fixed. The tracks are the limits, the lines of adventure. They confine, but do not suppress; they have direction and enclose space, but what they enclose is open and free. Much can be achieved between them. We can imagine that they are surpassed and suppressed. The leap into the vastness of the unknown terrifies and chastises. Man refrains from the leap; it plays havoc with his humanity which lies between the tracks. If the leap is possible, then what lies in the between remains only a part of his reality.

A scholar injected a new thought by saying that "when a writer bends over his work, he believes, or rather makes us believe, that his face is the one his words reflect. He is lying. He is lying as God would be if He claimed to have created man in His image; because which then would

---

[9]Ibid., 56-57.
[10]Ibid., 57.

be His image?"[11] We have repeated for generations the belief that we are created in the image of God, but we understood what this analogy meant. At one extreme we sought to maintain our closeness to God, and with glee allowed ourselves the privilege of assuming that we can do as he does. We are minor gods with capacities to act and create like the divine. But there were those who wisely wondered if we granted ourselves this lofty image, would there not be little difference between ourselves and God? We could now ascribe to God on a major scale what we have ascribed to ourselves on a minor one, and who would object if slowly but surely we narrowed the gap? But we could not do otherwise. At the other extreme we often found it necessary to widen the gulf between the mortal and the immortal to such a degree that the word *image* had little meaning. The sinful nature of man condemned him to a dualism which gave ontological status to evil, making it impossible to bridge the abyss which separated God and evil. One had to be destroyed in order that the other could survive. Often in reading the neglected Books of Kings we find the worship of Moloch, the sacrifice of children. The punishment is always God's wrath against Manasseh, Amon, and even Solomon, a wrath that is destruction. No reform is possible where death is the only consequence. The image of Moloch is an idolatry which can be used wherever we seek to comprehend the depths of evil. Moloch worship has never ceased, its transformative powers destroy man's humanity. "And I will set My face against that man and will cut him off from among his people, because he gave his offspring to Moloch and so defiled My sanctuary and profaned My holy name" (Lev. 20:3-4). In Moloch worship not only man but also societies and nations experience their decay and begin to envision their ruins.

At this point another scholar spoke these words: "Between thought and word, between the unforeseen dream and the foreseen syllable, there is the call of the roads we will take some day to tame the flaring passion which consumes us."[12] The poet leaves us with contradictions of perspectives and visions, but there are deeper ones which are indicated with the thought of the divine image. It is the loss of this image, or the reality of its nonexistence, that causes us to tremble and be terrified by our existence. The worship of Moloch points not only to hedonistic idolatry, but also to children and their sacrifice. The family is destroyed. Life is put into the arbitrary will of individuals. God and the creation are set aside in order that man can assume total domination of life. In the sacrifice of the child the foundation of familial life is ended. Man is no longer man. The poet doesn't take us into this horrific realm. He refuses

---

[11]Ibid.
[12]Ibid.

to defile the human reality. For Jabès the poetic dream remains alive. It is the last vestige of man's hope for redemption. The contrasts must remain between "unforeseen dream and foreseen syllable."

A scholar now interrupted, and said: "Adventure is in the service of the writer's need to live his words and to pursue the experience of life, to listen and to break through silence. Adventure he accepts and settles for because it is, at the same time, receiving a gift and showing it, a time of sowing and of harvest."[13] We are profoundly moved by what we see and hear, but these experiences remain empty without the pen. Writing opens to us a new experience hardly touched in sight or listening. The adventure of the pen brings with it the mystery of the mind, and we are aware that the seen and the heard are transfigured by the words of the thinking I. The I brings with it memory, reminiscences of realms that are dormant and must be revived. They startle us as they emerge to remind us of ideas forgotten and seemingly lost. Writing forces us to recognize how much has been lost, and is, therefore, not available to us. Each writing is a struggle between the lost and the found, the recallable and the dormant. We remain happily unknown to ourselves, and each piece of work is only a segment of our reality hopefully awakening others. "By the trickery of the word," as scholars told us, "man is and is not. The word, however, remains the word, this is to say, man's only chance to be or not in All and in Nothing."[14]

A scholar contributed these words: "Man fashions himself in the word. He continues to live his birth – We are born tomorrow – The death of man gives birth to the word through which man asserts and dismisses himself. The death of God in the book has given birth to man."[15] "We are born tomorrow" because we will be born again. Tomorrow will take us beyond time. It will stand against, and challenge, the birth of the day. We realize that tomorrow is possible only because today is the reality from which everything emerges. There can be no future without a past and a present. History depends upon the death of the past and the present. Men and events become words in a continuity that is hidden in death. The death of God becomes a wonder for man. He speaks of the divine image, the responsibility for creation, and of a divine-human dialogue. God's absence becomes the source of man's presence. God's presence was man's death. We needed to become creators, to write books, build temples, to sculpture and paint. The image of God allowed us to enter his realm and act with majesty and dignity. The human adventure slides

---

[13]Ibid.
[14]Ibid., 58.
[15]Ibid.

along with man not knowing how divine he is or how devilish he has shown himself to be.

Yukel said that "the Jew is so much subject to his name that he can never shake it off. If trunk, he is roots in the shape of a trunk. If branch, he is roots in the shape of branches. If fruit, he is a knot of energy. He runs where others walk; he swims where others float on their backs. He travels a long road. He is tripped in his dash. Killed like a dog. In a manuscript, he is no more than an awkward word to be crossed out."[16] From Yukel the parable and paradox of the Jew. The traveler who belongs to eternity but cannot live in it, he searches for his God and knows that his presence would destroy him. The absence of his God is the beginning of his life. The Jew seeks to form a state, but even there he wanders. His belonging is uncertain. The absence of his God allows him to be a man among men, to create a state among states. This he willingly accepts, but there is a destiny that drives him beyond borders, that allows him to dream dreams, to live paradoxes. He knows that he belongs to a people that dwells above, a people apparently like other peoples, but a people different from the others. The world is uneasy with Israel. The tribe has survived, the desert has survived in it. This is a people who is stiff-necked, and who refuses to find comfort in the faiths of others. It remains committed to the Fathers and their wanderings. The others look upon it with suspicion and fear. Its courage keeps Israel from assimilation. It wants to assimilate and does it well, but again and again it is spurned, reminded that in solitude it possesses its fate.

A guest enters the conversation and remarks: "When one Jew tells another why he had to leave his country, the listener thinks: He suffered in his country and now he has come to suffer in mine. And in the new exile's eyes there is always this question to the friend who took him in: Tell me, will I suffer as much here as I did in the country I come from?"[17] The concept of exile belongs both to historical reality and to the realm of Ideas. Adam is exiled from paradise, Abram from the land of his father. We are summoned to leave, to go, to wander in search of a new land. The land is either a new country or a new reality with new dreams and visions. The spirit needs to wander. It recognizes only momentarily its physical land, a time and a historical situation. The spirit is called upon to find a new path. It dwells only temporarily in a place, in a time. Its land is always beyond the immediate. It rejects identification with the immediacies of political and intellectual life, knowing that only in nonidentification is there that precious distance between the spirit and existence. The exile of the spirit is the life of the spirit. It wanders in the

---

[16]Ibid.
[17]Ibid., 59.

moving sands of the desert, in the ever-changing forms which beckon images and deepen our dreams.

The exile is also physical. It struggles with the change of lands, traditions, and language. The power of adjustment staggers the imagination; many succeed, while others fail to find new homes and travel about in confusion and disorder. Exile is not the end of a pain, nor is it the suppression of alienation. New lands bring new pain and alienation. The exiled spirit is always in danger. There is no salvation for the exiled. He is wounded physically and spiritually. Exile brings forth exile. Where there is an end, there we encounter lethargy and death. Death is the suppression of exile. The exile dies in identification and surrender. Physical death is only the conclusion to many spiritual deaths. Death is always levels of dying. Life makes us aware how intimate and close death is. It is the companion of life.

A scholar arose and spoke about the word: "A word," he said, "joins other words in order to further first of all the sentence, then the page, and finally the book. In order to survive it must take an active part in freeing the world of speech, must be a dynamic agent of its transformation and unity."[18] We are reminded constantly of the quality and power of the word as if this is a reality which must not be forgotten. To forget is to prepare for the transformation of the word into jargon, to defile man's most precious gift, which like many others is the source of his destruction. The word unites us with humankind. It lies at the foundation of the human community. The word is the bridge revealing to each of us the source of man's creativity. We think of the Bible becoming the book of humankind through Greek, and then in the multitude of other languages. Knowing how precious the word is forces us to face the powers of distortion that use it for the purposes of evil, for the lapidary language which captures the spirit and prepares its death. The word weaves the delicate combination of thoughts into poems, essays, and books. The word hovers over the word, points it in new and different directions, asking us to travel with it to new metaphors, to poetic reveries, and dreams. Where the word is alive others cluster around it. They live from it. The word in its intimacy with other words is never confined to a definition. It steps back with fear from the formulas which we attempt to mold with it. But the word is not free of our dominance.

A scholar added to the conversation a perceptive remark. He stated that "what moves or excites us in formulated thought is precisely its destruction as thought and its resurrection in the word."[19] We read this

---

[18]Ibid.
[19]Ibid., 60.

thought several times and we become aware that it embodies a distinctive truth. Rather than hearing the thought and using it as an instrument for capturing the world, we turn toward the words that form it and discover that the they do not necessarily provide the thought with its commanding capacity to give meaning to reality. In fact, the words emerge as forces that shatter the thought. We have to read again, listen again, and hear new tones and rhythms. The words that create a thought can equally destroy it. The words which move us in one direction have the capacity to direct us toward another. It is the word that emerges victorious in thought. Thought is its product, and is contingent upon the word. The word is always more than its product.

The word stands before us as the supreme instrument of our humanity. It is our humanity, the source of its expression, its beauty and sublimity. The word is the form we have giving hints of the indwelling divine. In the word we find traces of the divine image. In the word we suppress the image. We utter the word with indifference. We express it in the rituals of idolatry, in loyalty to ideology. With the word we bear witness to the spirit. With it we confess the evil that has tainted our nature.

A guest broke in and observed: "The Jew goes toward the Jew who waits for him, pushed by what he thinks his inescapable fate – which is nothing but people's fury to destroy him."[20] The word is embodied in history and its vocabulary. It reveals the history of Jewish fate. The word testifies to Jewish suffering and glory, and gathers together the strands of one and the other, showing how deeply dependent they are upon each other. The word comes together with words, unveiling a history of exile and suffering, of courage and stubbornness. In all these realities, the word remains unidentified, yielding glimpses into the unexplained and unknown, the enigmatic and mysterious quality which veils every human adventure.

Yukel returned and offered this comment: "Society often has as much contempt for thought as for Jews. Poets give words a chance to live with their dreams. They allow them souls. Sentimentally I feel close to the persecuted word because it is of my race. My revolt is hatching inside of me. My writings grow out of this revolt: across the words I aim at the tyrant."[21] We are deeply aware of how significant it is to give to words their right to dream, to give them a second or third life. The poet preserves as he guards the word, giving it the soul it has had for generations. The poet is the preserver of the word, keeping it within the tradition. He is the conservative, even the reactionary, who refuses to

---

[20]Ibid.
[21]Ibid., 60.

allow the word to be lost in the medley of jargon. If we speak of the European tradition, of an Anglo-Saxon community, then it is from the word that this tradition emerges and defends its right to be. The exiled and the persecuted know this well. In Jabès's work this preservation of the tradition is the overwhelming fact. The poet is the wanderer from the desert to the book, from the book to the desert, and he carries in his dream the book which was before the beginning. The poet questions the questions, knowing that the answers fall to other answers. The poet gives words to the soul, allowing it to speak its stories, telling of their destiny, revealing to us how they have formed our civilization.

The last scholar who spoke said: "Perhaps there will come a day when words will destroy words for good. There will be a day when poetry will die. It will be the age of the robot and the jailed word. The misery of the Jew will be universal." And Yukel commented: "The misery of the Jews will disarm misery."[22] I am only the word. How else do I express my humanity? I am the ceaseless questioner. From the beginnings of my travels I have speculated about the heavens and the earth. Questions have nurtured my soul and have never freed me from their grip. Unless the tyrant slays me, I remain the questioner. In my questions I explore and discover my reason and my will. Even when I act from commitment, I am never freed of the pursuing questions. I attempt to preserve my answers, but my questions gnaw at them, and my answers crumble. Quickly I search for new ones, but I know they also will be attacked and will disappear. I am free in this journey through questions and answers. Without them I would become a robot, my being would be jailed within a mechanism. My death is in the captivity of my question, and the domination of the answer. Where the answer destroys the question, there I feel the death of my being. I am a being who is accounted for on the lists, but who has died. Many a living being has died but is accounted for among the living. But this has not been the fate of the Jew; his misery increases his identity. In it he is held ever closer to his God. The Jew disarms misery because he has learned to enhance his stubbornness. In stubbornness the Jew found salvation. His stubbornness is his perseverance. This perseverance is the mystery of the Jew.

The conversation is over. It has taken us on many levels. We are shadowed by the thought that "there will come a day when words will destroy words for good." That day is too much for us to imagine and we set it aside, but it does not go away; it remains with us as a voice that never ceases to remind us that our destiny is filled with violence. Our fate remains undecided. We submit to no necessity but that of our own mortality and its freedom. But this freedom is neither an instrument of

---

[22]Ibid., 61.

good nor of evil; it moves in one direction or the other. No God will redeem us, and the fates have not finally condemned us. Man's misery is his freedom. Nothing terrorizes him more deeply than the power of choice. It "burns his lips" like the words of God. It is in freedom that man finds divinity, the hints and signs which the divine left in the world. Man knows that he is nothing more than his questions and answers, his search for the book, and the words that accompany it. The conversation has settled nothing; it never intended to. The scholars have not even spoken to each other. They have spoken their thoughts. The reader passes from one to the other, from one scene to another. There is nevertheless a harmony among these scenes. It lies in the word that speaks of a human reality. The scenes are housed in a single reality: the word and its endless forms, tones, and rhythms.

There is no conclusion, and we have no need of one. In Jabès's *The Book of Resemblances*, volume 2, we hear these words: "A page of dark on a page of light and so on ad infinitum, this is what our books are, said Reb Assouad. 'Out of Your book mine will be born tomorrow. Thus You shall be my reader, Lord, as I have always been yours.' Reb Assam had written. But Reb Salsel replied: 'There is no Book of God outside the book of man. It is your own book, Reb Assam, that you read in God's.' Did not Reb Hakim write: We try to read the book of God and, from the first word, realize that it is our own book God invites us to decipher?"[23]

There is no parting thought for the reader, but the experience of the word, the hearing, the seeing, and the poetic reverie. These are the experiences of each man who holds dearly to the word as the sacred possession of his being, who knows that each book is destroyed in order that a new one is engendered, which in its turn is overcome. The word is eternal and each book is a moment of its manifestation. Each book is a resemblance of the eternal, which dies with the sacrifice of the book and lives in the new book. With the poet each of us lives the movement from resemblance to eternity and from eternity to resemblance. We find in the book the desert and its unending forms, but no book can contain the desert, and therefore each book brings forth another book. The human journey wanders between the invisible and visible. We love the invisible through the visible and the visible through the invisible. Each poet who walks this paradoxical path knows that movement is always varied and undefinable. The journey we make yields no knowledge, but only parables. With these we seek to find parabolic meanings, which leaves us with new parables. These we can never surrender without losing our freedom, the imaginative powers of our being. We give answers only to

---

[23]*The Book of Resemblances*, vol. 2 *Intimations The Desert* (Hanover: University Press of New England, 1991), 22-23.

go beyond them. We question to surpass the question. Our wandering is our fate. We can only smile. We need to go forward.

7

The Exilic Wanderer

"A book has always for its background the agony of a book."[1] Agony fills the search of a book for a book, its search of a people, its search for the love which will unseal its seals, open the world to words, to sublimity and beauty. We have meditated with the poet upon the book and its concealment. We want the book to be everything. The book is nothing. We search in vain in our longing for everything. Everything takes us away from the book whose reality is its nothingness, the source of all things. We share with Jabès the love of the book. We share with him the love from which all books emerge, and to which they return after their venture to find the face of universe. The book is both Yaël and Elya. The book is a new sign for Yaël, one that belonged to her as the love of man for woman, one that excited the love that joins and separates, the love that yields the child but is not the child. We move slowly through *The Book of Questions,* the odyssey of the book, and we realize that we are journeying through an epic of love. This epic takes on many forms; it has no particular story to tell, only hints and directions for many poems and aphorisms. The reader writes love poems as he or she reads the words. He is aware that the poet has left him wide and white margins. Our voyages with Jabès reveal a sense of beauty, a balance of form and formlessness. Thought is called forth to be thought, to accompany what has been said by what must continue to accompany it: poem for a poem, commentary for commentary, image for image. We cannot read Jabès without writing about what we have read, composing as he has composed. Jabès invites companionship. The reader walks with him, speaks with him, and discovers that there is poetry within him, the capacity to create forms and to join them with those of the poet. We

---

[1]*The Book of Resemblances,* vol. *I* (Hanover: University Press of New England, 1990), 21.

cannot read Jabès like an object which can be described and analyzed. We read him if we can converse with him, and write the poetry that lives in us.

The book of Elya begins with these words about the book: "In back of the book there is the ground of the book. In back of the ground there is immense space and, hidden in this immense space, the book we are going to write in its enigmatic sequences."[2] The book dwells in paradoxes and is revealed in parables. The book is the foundation of the book. We long for its presence, and discover that its presence is its absence. Where there is an idol, there is no book. In the idol matter becomes demonic, it loses its limitations, the temporary quality of its being. The book denies the demonic quality of the idol. In relationship to the book, human nature reveals its finiteness. The book causes man to be dissatisfied, to realize that there are vast perspectives of the universe that are open to his exploration. The presence of the book crushes the limitation which man sets to his world and to the self. The book is grasped when it is no longer the book, when it fades away in our grasp. It slips through the comprehension and is lost in the definition. Where the book is assumed to be revealed, there we find the demise of the book. But what then is the book? The poet has taken us on many journeys. We have searched for the presence of the book, but it is always beyond us, escaping into the labyrinth. Man attempts to open a path to the book through the word. The word is the carrier of the book, but it is also the death of the book. We find life and death in the book. We long to hang onto the word, but our very longing becomes its death.

For generations men have sought to discover their relationship to the book. They knew that the book existed from the beginning, that it was the foundation of poetry, of universal speculation. It drove men to discover their imagination, to realize that what is present to the eyes, the ears, the taste, reveals and hides what is before us. Human life remains a metaphysical mystery, and it is this mystery which has given it its poetry and its arts, its sciences and technologies. When we put the mysterious aside, when we open life exclusively to reason and definition, when we struggle for a conquest over the unknown, we bring about the victory of death. The domination of the known over the unknown is the death of life. Life needs to remain incomplete, to affirm its unending reality, the limitless limits of creative powers. Beyond every moment of the known lies new possibility, a gracious and open journey into the unexplored and unvisited realm of life, the realm of the book.

"It seemed obvious to you," the poet remarked, "that after the day you would think of conjuring up the night, that after having read words,

---

[2]*The Book of Questions*, 5:121.

you would think of silence. But you could not interfere with the unfolding of your work. Each of its pages had to use its guaranteed right to its own death. And so the book would disappear in the book."[3] The wonder of work is the movement from control to domination. We feel the powers of the thinking I, commanding the writing and images which come forth from it. But the writing has powers which dominate thought, giving it an inexplicable movement. We think, we analyze, and we believe that we comprehend. It is only in writing that we discover what we have read and thought. There lies the mystery, the discovery of the thinking I, which is not in itself but in its expression, in what was unpredictable and unknown. This is the mystery that hovers over man and his work. Man is the being who believes that he is free, but who is free only in the reality of his work, in what he does and what he creates.

But we must think of the book disappearing in the book. We must think of man's work finding its truth in what is beyond his work. Death is man's redemption from the idolatry of self-sufficiency. Death reveals the finiteness of man, his bond to time and space. Finiteness is man's fate. But finiteness is limit, the fate of limit. There is always the presence of the book. "My truth in the book is my truth outside life. Thus my life grows around my books. I write by the light of what is not revealed in what I express."[4] Here we touch the mystery which permeates every creative act, the light which draws our soul from itself toward the foods which come to it from the above and the beyond. Our journeys with Jabès have always taken us from the earth to the heavens, from the human to the divine. We feel absorbed by the light and darkness which dwell within our thoughts, the presence and absence of the eternal book which is both silence and voice. Jabès showed us how powerful is that light which dwells in our expression, and is yet beyond it, revealing to us the interplay of life and death which is present in all that we do. Death has never been the enemy of life, but its source and salvation. It is our salvation from idolatry. Things and beings die. Our spiritual works die, but they are the foundation of the continuous creation of the spirit. We create with pen and brush because others have done the same. We seek new expressions because we need to be more than links in a chain. We want to live in new worlds, and from different perspectives, but so much of what we do is bound to time. We know that much of what we create will die. Life struggles to survive, to create, to bring forth new works. What would remain of our longing to work if death did not sweep away much of what we achieved? Life is the consequence of the cleansing power of death. Death deprives us of our autonomy, of our self-love, of

---

[3]Ibid., 125.
[4]Ibid., 125-26

the wish to preserve for eternity what we create. Death guarantees the
will to create.

"Life," the poet said, "always comes *after* the book, as being comes
after the face, *after* the landscape where we observe, meditate, or love."[5]
Life is not autonomous. It is dependent upon a reality greater than itself.
Life comes *after* the book. Something must tell us what life is. It is the
book which tells us about life. It is the book which tells us about death.
The book is both life and death. Man's life in the world is a commentary
on hope and despair, dream and vanity, vision and hesitation. The
finiteness, which we call life, gives pause to all that we do, but this
finiteness is not in life. It is what we impose upon it. We have said that
finiteness is fate, but fate is given to life by man. Whatever man imposes
upon life comes from his experiences and traditions. The truth of life,
however, lies in the book. There is no such truth for man. This is the
truth of concealment. Each truth which man assumes comes forth from
his experience of time, from the spatial immediacy of events. Man
identifies truth with his momentary experience. Man seeks to absolutize
these experiences, to destroy the flow of time. These absolute experiences
become man's idols. The presence of the book forces us to measure all
experiences by transcendence, by what they are not, by death, by the
powers of life to be reborn from the ashes of death. The symbol of life is
the phoenix.

"Between me and myself," the poet observed, "there are
innumerable words whose ways and will I do not know. They move me
away from the book which, sentence by sentence, has moved away from
them."[6] How little I know of myself as I meditate upon what I do and
think! There are so many words which are unclear and difficult to
comprehend. Writing does not allow me to clarify myself to myself; it
leaves me with a vast realm of uncertainty which I have no capacity to
measure or control. Writing makes me aware of the unknown before,
and within, me. It draws me away from the book. There are words which
give me new directions, show me new visions and images. Words lead
us astray and we are carried along by their intoxication. We feel like sea
voyagers in the heavy surf, moving from side to side, stirred only by
excitement and fear. Words have given us the lapidary slogans of racism
and political clichés. They have become the idols and terms of ideologies
which permeate both democracies and dictatorships. Such words move
us away from the book which remains the gift of the unknown to man's
violent search for universal knowledge. The book is the death of this
search, the light which reveals the limitations of human forms and

---

[5]Ibid., 126.
[6]Ibid.

desires. In the presence of the book, man's schemes for universal
knowledge reveal their sources in man's finiteness. The book restrains
man's longing for divinity. The majesty and holiness of the book
confuses man's search to regain the tree of life. The book shows man the
lessons of the phoenix, the profound interplay of life and death, of glory
and failure. We need the ashes of life to gird us for the struggle to unlock
the powers of death.

"Becoming conscious of death," Jabès noted, "means denying any
hierarchy of values which does not account for the stages of darkness
where man is initiated into the mysteries of the night. Death is both the
loss and the promise of a hope which day wears itself out courting at
every moment. To be or not to be in the absurd agony of a secret glimmer
until morning."[7] How deeply does the consciousness of death permeate
the religious soul of man? This question emerges from the realization
that death is the pivotal problem of religious life. The religious life is
filled with the challenge of death, "the mysteries of the night." So deeply
tied to death is life, so inexplicable is death to human existence, so
powerful is its mystery, that every religion has meaning for its believers
when it attempts to convey to them the meaning and overcoming of
death. The reality of death necessitates revelation and redemption. The
domination of the reality of death gives to life a new and vast dimension.
We have no intention of presenting the realities of life and death as
ontological absolutes, creating an irreconcilable dualism. To speak of life
embraced in death or of death embraced in life is to speak
metaphysically. The vision of the interrelationship is metaphysical but
also religious. The problem is announced in the epiphany: "I am who I
am." There are no other words we can use to reveal the divine. Man
must say: I am who I am and who I am not. Man affirms being. He
declares nonbeing not to be. He declares the reality of nonbeing, the flux
of all things which is the law of human life. Where there is flux, there is
human existence; where there is identification, there is the divine. Flux is
death and life. It is the mystery of their relationship. Death returns
everything to ashes. Life redeems the ashes, and from them life is again
the precious substance alive in death.

"In the schoolyard, recess is in full swing. But who is this child who
chooses to be off to the side, who is dreaming – looks as if he is dreaming
– propped against the wall? His name is Elya, a boy of the same age tells
his playmate. Ah, says the other. Too bad for him. They stared at him for
a brief moment, then forgot."[8] In Elya, there is silence, the tranquillity of
the desert. In him there is the dream, the birth of a new world, the death

---

[7]Ibid., 34.
[8]Ibid., 127.

of an old world. This is how the relationship of one upon the other makes us aware of their dependency. Elya belongs to the dream, to that death which removes a life to bring forth a new life. This it does without weapon and terror. This it does in the spirit which dies and lives in poetic reveries. In the ancient image of the phoenix we have, in spoken and unspoken words, the movement of the spirit. We have presence and absence, silence and the word, life and death. These opposites have their dwelling in Elya. We feel their dwelling as we meditate upon the passing of life and the presence of death. The more we are aware of "the mysteries of the night," the more delicate and full of wonder is the life we possess. But death is equally precious. It removes from us life forms which must pass away. Man's sin lies in his desire to preserve what he has always known to be life, in his fear of new forms, his fear of entering into new realms of being. Man's fear of death is his fear of life. He captures and captivates what he possesses, gives it absolute forms, and thinks of it as totality. Man fears spiritual change. He fixes and defines his religious faith. He puts it in forms of dogmas. He finds security in them. He finalizes God's word and repeats the sayings of his fathers. They become the songs of repetition, the chants of history.

Nothing lies more deeply in the soul of man than the consciousness of death. From this consciousness man reaches out to the divine. In God he finds redemption from death, but death cannot be redeemed. Where death is redeemed, life dies. The overcoming of death returns man to God. Man redeemed from both life and death has died unto life. He calls this redemption, eternal life, a vision which is neither life nor death. Man struggles for life. His struggle is against eternity, against the overcoming of death. Man's struggle is against the religious belief in the death of death. Man needs to know that "under the ashes there is homage to fire which you can hear."[9] Human life is embodied in contradictions, in the love which permeates and emerges from them. Human life is born from its negation. Every moment of this life must be suppressed and born again. We are children of growth and change. Our spirit needs time and space. It needs to evolve from form to form. Every year of life is change and disorder, development and creation.

We heard from the poet words that challenge our reason. He told us: "Man is All. God is Nothing. Here is the riddle. To glide towards Nothing. Perennial Slope."[10] In the dialogue of contradictions, man discovers the totality of human life, but there is always the Nothing which is at the limits of the All. This Nothing disturbs and threatens the All, gives lie to its totality, turns man from its completeness and causes

---

[9]Ibid., 128.
[10]Ibid.

him to wonder about the interplay of life and death. The Nothing is the limit of the human reality. In the limit we discover a yearning for the Nothing. Here lies the wonder that is embraced by human life, the dissatisfaction which causes life to surpass itself, "to glide towards Nothing." But this path toward Nothing is perilous. In Nothing, life is submerged and destroyed. Man finds in it his demise.

Jabès told a story about the book which he had heard from a sage: "The book, I was told by a sage I sincerely respected, contains a face we wrinkle in writing. The older the book, the purer the face. And he added: Do not believe that the book (which is not spared illness) disappears with the book. It dies only in its filigree. We know it is up to us to look for it beyond where it will give us back our written world. He said further: A lake is at the peak of power because it is master over the reflection which haunts it. Likewise the book when it lets us hear and drink."[11] We hear the story about the book, and we have heard many stories, but none brings us close to the book. The book is like the sands which we hold and whose drift we feel through our fingers. We know nothing and everything about the book; we know only that it is there within us and beyond us. The book is close to us. We write commentaries and endless books, attempting to embrace and define the book. The book is always there in our books, and always absent from them. The book is pure; the whiteness of its margins attracts our pen and we fill them with words. We always want to breathe the pureness of the book onto our pages. We will never cease to draw the purity of the book toward the impurity of our writings. Why can't we stop thinking of the book? Why does it not let go of our thoughts? Why does it not let us find our peace among the contradictions we know to be life? We are mysteriously drawn to the book, its purity and untouchability. The book is the Nothing which limits the All of human life. We are free before the book. We have no authority to ask what the book is. We stand face to face with the book. There is no place where the book doesn't have its presence.

"When he realized that the Word had a face and that Silence had one likewise, he understood that man, in what he introduces or keeps unsaid, has now the face of God, now that of His absence."[12] With wondrous fears and tremblings, we realize the faces of God and the silence which they bear. We confront both mystery and incomprehension in the face of the book. Through this face we perceive the glory and magnificence of man; through silence these qualities become obscure and fade away. They return to the hidden God who has lost himself in death and reveals himself in the Word as concealment. God lives as life and death in man.

---

[11]Ibid., 131.
[12]Ibid., 134.

Man remains a mystery to himself. He has in himself the presence of the absent God. Man's magnificence is his distortion. His sublimity and beauty emerge in ugliness and vulgarity. We realize that the changes are natural, and we feel pained to learn how quickly face changes face. But these are realities we need not explain. Explanations are of little consequence for us. We need to know that Cain is Abel's brother and Abel lives in Cain. We need to know that mankind lives with the two faces of man. These two faces are not separable from each other. They dwell with each other in struggle and envy. Where we find hints of the divine, we find the silence of the divine. Nothing is in solitude. Man, is the realm of conflicting opposites which make his life possible. Man seeks to escape the blindness which occurs with the domination of either God or silence. Where there is light, there is darkness. Where there is beauty, we find distortion. The light blinds us, beauty distorts us. How gracious we are when each is a limit for the other.

The poet related a tale: "God she had said to me. I carried him in my belly close to nine months. When those violent contradictions and cramps, of more than my flesh, announced the hour of His birth, everything around me died. God was dead with the birth of the child."[13] We wander with the poet into the labyrinth of obscurity and we wonder if this is where he wanted us to go. The closeness of the relationship between man and God brings with it the other question of their distance and separation. We walk on one rail as we walk on the other. Distance and closeness are intimately related. The birth of God brought death to everything which surrounded it. The presence of God is the death of humanity. The birth of man is the death of God. Here we face the most agonizing contradiction. We seek the divine as liberation from our humanity, but we also seek the divine as liberation from divinity, from the subservience of the spirit to the divine. We are children of the paradox. We are tellers of parables. However we want to tell our story, whatever narrative we decide to employ, we cannot escape the contradictory directions our life must follow. The narrative of man reveals the paradoxical search for the God who is his death. But man must search for God. Without this search, human life becomes idolatry. It finds its beginning and end in itself. Man is painfully theomorphic. Human life is insufferable without the hope for salvation; but salvation is the demise of man. Human life before the presence of God is the redemption of contingency and accident. They give life its richness and freedom. Man tells his story through conflict and contrast, in love and solitude. He tells his story in the presence of Abel and Cain. The shades

---

[13]Ibid.

of contrast reveal the quality of human life. The brightness of the divine light blinds the eyes. The tongue burns with the words of God.

"What comes about," the poet asked, "without the word, in the spoken word? Perhaps you? Perhaps me? Perhaps the world."[14] Where there is the word, there is not necessarily the spoken word. This distinction is of great significance, particularly for those who deify the word, for those who refuse to imagine the death of God at the creation. God is always a witness to his own death, freeing himself from man's search to find him in the self, from definitions and narratives which enclose and captivate him. God dies before man's imperial powers to proclaim the autonomy and completeness of his own reality. God dies within himself. His manifestation dies, but divine forms lead to divine forms. For man the longing to hold onto a particular form and to declare its sanctity and totality is idolatry. God dies in man's hands as he dies in every particular form of manifestation. Man's world slips through the divine reality. Man yearns to identify it with the Word, but there is no such identification. The Word surpasses man, and leaves vents in the crevices and cracks of humanity. The poet causes us to journey through lands untouched by the authorized narratives and histories. His voice leads us through realms strange to thought and imagination. We are aware of new modes of expressions, new paths of travel, new images, and new dreams. We live with surprise and fascination. The imagination is excited as we remove the clothing of tradition. The old clothing is put aside and new vestments prepared for us. These are the vestments of the individual facing God. Even these will become old, and we are conscious of a change which is ceaseless and piercing. The columns of permanency crumble. The new vistas are the preparations for future explorations. The poet leads us from realm to realm, becoming in each a more subtle and startling guide. The poet is transfigured into the spiritual string which we follow out of the labyrinth of habit and authority. He now emerges as a radiant light who shows us the stars in the "mysteries of the night."

"I speak...," said the poet, "but to whom? And why speak? For whom? How? With what aim, in which light, which perspective? To speak – under what pretext, to which end? Ah, to go up to where and where from? To stop at which frontier, in which dark or flame, on which beach or mountain?"[15] We are touched by painful questions, ones from which we ourselves cannot escape. The wise man cannot hide under the shell of the turtle. We have no shell. We have only the openness of the heavens, the vastness of the desert, and the limitless exile. There is no place to find the dwelling which shelters us from the starry heavens and

---

[14]Ibid., 136.
[15]Ibid.

the unending dunes. Our words have lost their connections with things. We have been exiled from the garden. Our words are only mediations, bridges which we try to build between ourselves and our fellowmen. The word has gone with us into exile. It is an exiled word. We struggle with the word and the word expands and contracts to fulfill our longings to link the human and the divine. The word has become man's tool and speaks a nomadic language. We are wanderers, dwelling where we pretend to find the permanency of rest. The spirit wanders and finds no rest. Wherever the spirit is, it finds dissatisfaction and needs to wander to new lands and sights. Our conversations are temporary and we find momentary commentaries to satisfy the needs of our reason. We speak of the permanency which would have left us tranquil and peaceful, but this is our death. In exile we speak exilic words. We create momentarily for the tastes and habits of our age. The exile allows us to construct the historical narrative. This is the tale of a life of wonder, of metaphysical disquietude. We look forward and upward. In all directions we find paths, and we travel learning how to live and wonder, how to settle and how to leave. The spirit is restless. In his perplexity, man finds the sadness of his glory and of his fate. Man is a nomad.

"To speak – under what circumstances, after what silence, wave, or incomparable path in midocean, after what question, desert, exile, before what dawn? I speak – in what summer, after what long winter, what call, what failure, before what scream? – after what death, before what death?"[16] We know no longer when to speak. We realize that our words are heard and not heard. Our words are forgotten and ring only in our ears. The world runs mad with its search for fixed forms. Man would like to create again a language which is identical to the things they designate. He seeks to formulate philosophies whose truths belong to their language. The deified language attracts and enchants man. He would like to make it his dwelling, end his exile, and find again the lost garden. This search dooms man and those around him. It cuts off the freedom which is alive only in doubts and questions. The word is precious to man. In it he hears the remembrances of his past, his poetry and philosophy, his arts and sciences. He hears the sounds of his nomadic wanderings, the movement of the desert sands. He sees the image of the phoenix, the ashes and the life that emerges from them. He stands before and after death. Death is his companion in life. Death causes him to speak of life, of the word which is expressive life, the word of the spirit, the word in which creativity is born. Man speaks only in the awareness of death. Knowing that life is easily destroyed, that he lives in exile and fades into the sands, man finds in the word the revolt of life, the

---

[16]Ibid.

manifestation of its vitality and productivity. The word is the salvation of life. The word is a chameleon. It is ours, but we are its servant.

Language enables us to speak from the exile in the sea, from the mountains and the desert. Wherever we are, in the streets of the city, in the wheat fields and among the flowers, we build with the word our relations to life and death. We are enticed by the powers of the world and we strive to make them comprehensive and embracing. We fall in love with the word and deify it. We forget that it is our instrument, commanded by our reason, inspired by our love. We fall prey to the word, become enchanted by it, and lose the distance between reason and its tool. The word is more than a tool. It charms and seduces its creator and puts him under its spell. The work and its maker belong to each other like lover and beloved. The word carries us to distant lands, to images that stir our imagination and make us aware of the poetry of reverie. The word takes us into the labyrinth of creativity and then leaves to be a wanderer. It leads us in, but doesn't carry us away. The poet remarked that "this desire to make what was into what is and, then, what is into what will last, leads us to supplant the human face by another which we want inviolable the better to encircle it."[17]

The poet showed us how man eagerly seeks to end his wandering, to find the relationship between his past, his present, and his future. Man is not only a wanderer, he is also the observer wherever man believes he has found certainty and rest. Man constructs religions to find certainty. He listens with pleasure to the voices of the orthodox and often to the fanatic. Man seeks security in political life; there he finds comfort in charismatic leadership and the cliché. In the sciences, man remains open to novelty because he is convinced that technology provides a better life. Man, the wanderer, had become a strange and tasteless reality to his fellowman. Spiritual exile and universality don't belong to a world in search of self-satisfaction. Man needs to supplant the threadbare face of exile with the defined and carefully delineated face of clarity and certainty. In this way man discovers the anonymity of modernity.

"God," Jabès said, "faces God, and the book the book. Night is cut off from the night by a light which burns it. Words stay forever separate. And the writer? He is like the earth which turns on itself and around a slower light whose near and far sides he explores. Like the earth, he would love to be the center of the universe."[18] Driven from the garden, man discovers the world of ruptures and resemblances. He discovers the world of man. Here his words hide words. His books give forth books. Nothing remains permanent. The question builds up on questions, and

---

[17]Ibid., 137.
[18]Ibid., 138.

the answers multiply endlessly. What Jabès cultivated in himself, he does not ask of his reader. Those who accompany him do not follow him. He is not a master who takes on disciples. For those around him, there are the empty spaces which they must learn to fill with books and commentaries, which in turn will have the whiteness of the virgin fields. With Jabès, the poet becomes the poet, the writer, the writer. They know that words live in the words, that what is put forth in the letters only resembles the things of which they speak and at the same time is differentiated from them. There is solitude and ubiquity and each speaks a language. "God leans on God, the book on the book, man on his shadow."

God, like the book, is ever present, but presence is always absence, as solitude is always communication. The one never appears without the other. Never is one separated from the other without distortion. This is the life of the spirit which gives birth to the desert, to God, and to the book. This is the spirit born from the desert, from the book, and from God. We are always questioning our journeys with Jabès; sometimes we wonder where we are going, and sometimes we wonder about the meaning of our travels. The book is always present, but it is not a defined book, a narrative of events which we can learn and then repeat. The book defies the claim of anything to become absolute and fixed. Everything belongs to change, a momentary experience measured by the eternity of the book. The book deprives us of our defined faith. It calls forth the imagination, and forces us to create new images rather than repeat the old ones. We move from experience to experience, knowing that the world is incomplete. We are men in search of journeys that are yet to be made. We are the poets of the aphorism. We have seen the crumblings of the systems. Men love to play God, to look at themselves and see the face of autonomy and freedom. But we are creatures of chance and arbitrariness. Jabès remarked that "the book is the place where a writer offers his voice up to silence. Hence, every margin is the breach of avowal held back. And on its edge, the words gather and seal their alliance with the sea. My bible is the page you cannot choose."[19]

The writer is a teller of tales. The tales, unlike the novel, leave much to tell. The tale that he has to tell brings us to the shores of the sea. There before us is the vastness of space, of tales yet to be told and the innumerable journeys yet to be taken. We love the poet because he has brought us here, away from our cities and their streets, away from the marketplaces and government offices where everything seems to be fixed and ordered. We need to walk away from the everyday events with their necessary beginnings, middles, and ends, and find the seas, the

---

[19]Ibid., 141.

deserts of our imagination. Our words become sounds and voices in space, and in the beyond of the everyday flow of time. We look back on this everyday existence and wonder how we live in it. But it is also life. We need to walk away and make an "alliance with the sea," with the unknown, the unexpected, and the imaginative. In that alliance, like the one God made with the world, we discover the possibility of creative life, the life of the spirit.

The "alliance with the sea" is the eternal binding between man, the invisible, and the impenetrable. Nothing arouses our love more deeply than the invisible. If religion has a place in our lives, it belongs to the invisible. We are in exile because of our love of the invisible. We did not determine our exile; it was determined for us by the invisible. The religious man is born from the "alliance with the sea." In it we find the mystery which brings forth the desert and makes us wander with the word. The book is the source of our exile. It cannot be fixed nor defined. The book guides us to the invisible, and leaves us surprised and bewildered by a love that is unceasing and insatiable. How quickly we flee this path and seek shelter in the defined and fixed word, in the narratives of tradition. How tired we grow with the myopia of the engraved word, stone imbedded in stone! God dies in God as the book dies in the book. We easily turn to the stone and feel secure in the dwelling. Our exile is over and we no longer die like the phoenix. Life is separated from death and death from life. Jabès journeys through the exile of the desert. We walk with him knowing that only in the desert will forms become formless, and sounds fade away into screams and howls, having no place and words.

Through all the wanderings and questions, Jabès remained attached to the fate of the Jews, to the eternal fate of a people whose God had become silence, whose presence became absence. Nevertheless, the Jew wanders with his absent God, who is there with him, in his absence. The Jew is free with his God. He never ceases to question him. This is the uniqueness of Jabès's journeys, the beauty and sublimity of his poetic vision and dreams: to wander alone with the silence and absence of God. Jabès noted: "The road taken by a Jew, some sage said, is the imperceptible course of a drop of water from the mountaintop to the sea. I will have been a Jew in my course.... I will have been a Jew for not being able to answer to any but myself, more of a stranger than anyone else, and to the poorest in the losing word."[20] Jabès was Jewish in a profound and distinct sense. He remained the poet of the original, the primordial experience of the desert, the voice, and the divine absence. The desert is the eternal image from and in which all images of

---

[20]Ibid., 142.

wandering and meditation emerge. The Jew is the consequence of the desert. He is a man of exile, belonging to no land, a stranger among peoples. He has made an alliance with the sea, the vastness and incomprehensibility of the invisible. He is in love with the invisible. He hears the voices of his past. They are the voices of the Fathers. He hears their faith and doubt, their loves and sufferings. He hears their sounds embodied in the book which is always being written, although it has been written. Jabès journeyed with the absent God, with the hovering and silence which made us aware of the power of absence. In God's absence, Jabès knew of his presence as labyrinth, as the Nothingness which encompasses the creation. Journeying in the divine silence is the odyssey of the spirit. There is no divine voice. Revelation becomes silence. Not what God is supposed to have said, but the silence hiding among his words is his truth. The poet doesn't assume to be a teacher of men. He is the teacher of teachers. His words do not come down as prescriptions and definitions. They come forth as paths, images, and journeys.

The Jew is "the homeless fruit of aggressive silence." We believe that in the exile of the soul, the Jew, like everyman, finds the book. The book reveals the fate of exile. It belongs to no place and to no time, it has no message and no words of wisdom. Its reality cannot be transformed into a prayer book. The book is the light and the darkness, it is the stars and the heavens. It is the nothing before, and in, creation. The book is the fate of the exilic wanderer. The poet brought the book to those who journey with him, who dream dreams and have visions. The book is the sacred possession of the perplexed. Where this perplexity fades into certainty, there the book fades. Jabès is the poet of the perplexed. For this reason we have continued our journeys with him. They are journeys calling into question all that we have known. We shake and tremble as we hear the scream of the book. We become aware of how deeply dependent we are upon it, its presence and absence, its voice and its silence.

The thinker, the poet, touches the mystery of exile, he testifies to the reality of absence in which life begins and ends. He reveals the being and nonbeing which is embodied in the word and in the self. He is the nomadic thinker. His way is *la pensée indéterminée* (undetermined thinking). Jabès is our guide, if in this realm a guide is possible. He is the companion with whom we speak and walk, with whom we wander into the desert, and watch the desert move into us. He is the companion with whom we find our love of the invisible, and hear the screams of the past. With Jabès, we walk, we listen, and form forms.

8

The Odyssey of the Exilic Wanderer

The spirit remains poor and negligible, alone in desolation and silence. The spirit is weak and sickly in its quietude and immobility. The spirit is dying in its inactivity and inseparability. The spirit breathes again when it stirs and moves, when it begins to wander, when it becomes nomadic, when it affirms the existence of the self and denies the things around it. In their nonexistence, the spirit has life. In exile, the spirit lives. It creates in the absence of being. The spirit stirs as it hears the words spoken to Abram: "Raise your eyes and look out from where you are, to the north and south, to the east and west, for I give all the land that you see to you and your offspring forever. I will make your offspring as the dust of the earth, so that if one can count the dust of the earth, then your offspring too can be counted" (Gen., 13:14-17). In the raising of his eyes, Abram turns away from what is about him, he looks to a new reality, to the stars and the heavens, to the darkness and the light, to the beautiful and the sublime. The spirit moves when its vision, encompasses the limits of the world. In these it finds its movement, its vision and its dream. In the lands of the east and the west, in those of the north and the south, the spirit wanders and finds the objects of its love, the foods of creativity. The spirit is a nomad. It knows no country and no people. It lives from their absence, i.e., from the absence which is present. The spirit is always *here* in political and moral existence, but it is also beyond, unidentified, alone, and free. The spirit belongs to a land but has no dwelling in it. The spirit lives in the invisible, the unknown and the unexpected. Where we claim to find it, to see it and possess it, it flees from us, it fades away, moving to new lands and new vistas. The spirit belongs to humankind, to the limits of the universe that are always beyond its limits.

Jabès observed that "at this time before time, when life was only a sickly death with weak lungs, one small point in space contained, like a

bubble, all the wanderings of the worlds. When it burst it freed the
universe, but gave form to exile."[1] There is no contradiction between the
freedom of the universe and the exile. The freedom of the universe lives
in the exile, in that wondrous bubble which contains the wanderings of
man, those which the divine held forth to Abram, the limitless visions
and dreams which belong to man's spiritual life. Jabès taught his
companions the love of the invisible, the contrasts of light and darkness,
the intimacy of life and death, the need which they have for each, and the
love which holds them together. The exile is the eternity of the human
spirit, a captive of no man, no nation, and no land. Men have always
sought to capture the spirit, imprison and delineate it. Men who call
themselves religious identify it with their traditions and habits. These
men become its priests, rabbis, and holy men. But the spirit moves
through walls, overflows the dwellings intended for its captivity is alive
again and in universality, in the light which gives light, in the death
which is the source of man's creative life. The spirit moves through
absence to the divine name. One small point is that qualitative moment.
It is that infinitesimally small point from which all qualitative moments
take their power. From the smallest to the greatest, it is the spirit which
brings forth life. The point must overcome the vast quantity which is the
universe. Into this vastness comes the spirit, a minute force of
transformation and transfiguration. In the minuteness of the spirit lives
the explosive force of creativity. Where in the vastness of the heavens, in
the obscurity of reality, dwells this infinite power which is the mystery
and the beauty of life? In the nonresponse live all responses.

"Never again will we escape exile" is a truth which we have not
imposed upon ourselves or the universe. It has been imposed upon us. It
is the fate of our finiteness, of our Jewish existence, of our love of the
desert. "Raise your eyes" are the words told to Abram. These are words
from which the exile begins. They are words of exilic contemplation. We
are not the children of nature, but those of the book, a book in exile. They
tear us away from what had become our natural dwelling. They send us
in new directions, to seek new journeys and new speculations. We are
always driven to new lands as long as the spirit is alive in us. Our fate is
our exile. A world must be denied, another must be given to us. The
image is the phoenix, the movement from life to death and from death to
life. But this is a free image. The world about us has lost its permanency
and validity. The poet lives in the world he creates, the images he forms
of it. The world is lost in concreteness. With that world, we have lost our
vitality and purpose. We need to look upon the world, to create it with
our words, with metonymy and metaphor. We need our imagination and

---

[1]"Elya," 144.

reason to find our way back to the spirit which hovers above us in exile. We take the exile into ourselves. This is man's decisive act: the embrace of exile, the exile embraced. How strange but how wondrous it is for man to long for exile, to loosen his bonds with space and time, to journey toward the invisible, knowing that in and through this travel man separates himself radically from his searches for a reality which is the absence of what is presence, becoming the presence of its absence. In the presence lives that delicate but forceful interrelationship between being and nonbeing, between the nuances, contrasts, and tones which inhabit the intricacies of human existence.

"A word without destiny, an unpronounceable name," the poet remarked, "was the floral ornament of our page."[2] The spirit comes between the self and the world. It has no purpose and no destiny. The spirit longs to be awakened. It is eager to separate us from the world about us and give us that mysterious distance between our imagination and experience of reality. The spirit remains unknown; no word is adequate to express its reality, no perception is able to reveal its powers of transformation. If we discover the depths of absence, of the powers to look toward the invisible, we find our capacity for negation and transfiguration. We find within the self that peculiar and distinct desire for metamorphosis. In this reality we experience the exile of the journey, the never-ending transfiguration of reality, the realization that there is a world of images and dreams lying behind the visible, lying behind the world and its empirical impressions. The world went into exile when man left the garden. It is this world which man seeks to recover in poetry. It is a world which he will never regain; his poetry is inadequate. The word is no longer God's. Man grasps only hints and signs and with these he goes forward in his unceasing exploration to find what is not discoverable, the hidden reality of God, who has died with his creation. Man finds the silence and absence of divinity. From this perspective the writer seeks to bring forth pure poetry, those relationships and sounds that he believes lie behind those which appear to him. No longer do we find or seek reality in what is before and with us, in the reflections which appear to us. Truth reemerges slowly and only with hints. We know that it is *there*, but we must help it to come forth. It must be touched and nudged with love and devotion. From the fallen world of appearances, we glimpse the word that lies unknowingly and obscurely within it.

"In other eyes," Jabès remarked, "being means becoming, whereas in ours, it means one day, having been. I am whatever bears my name and continues when I am interrupted. The world does not exist except in mysterious references to a past world. I do not exist except in relation to

---

[2]Ibid., 145.

the space of a word uttered."[3] The miracle of our existence belongs to the past, which bore within us our fate. What we have been is the reality which governs our life. The past bears a fate we cannot escape. It is a fate, we carry into the present and will carry into the future. Becoming for us means taking the past into the present and the future. There is no unburdening of the past. We may want to forget it, to drive it from our thoughts and feeling, but others remember it for us, and proclaim the past as our dwelling. The Jew does not escape the past which molded and has shaped his existence. He may wish to be swallowed and be forgotten, but fate pursues him. It reminds him of his destiny. Other men dream of a new future which will embody their past and their present. Their reality is yet to be born, their hopes are yet to emerge, and their dreams yet to be realized, but Jewish existence lives with the book, with reminders of the beginnings, their exiles and wanderings. From these, Jewish existence forms its presence and its future. It cannot look forward, without looking backward. The future was already promised in the past. The circle of return is perpetual. The journeys of the present must bear the promises and fate of the past. How these come forth and are manifested are the problems of the present. Each man takes up his travels alone. There are no given and formed responses to the past. Each man faces history alone, having only the responses of others which may or may not be guides. The wonder of Jewish existence is the freedom of the response, the way of solitude. How each individual takes on the past and responds to it is his freedom, his right to conversation and commentary.

My name comes from my conversations and commentaries. In them, I have formed my relationships with the world. In them alone, I acquire my ability to speak, to find a world that has meaning to me. Here I find those mysterious terms which allow me to construct my world. With my words, I construct my relationship to the past. I cannot simply repeat the words of others. I can be inspired and influenced by them, but I, in my solitude, must create my bonds. I form the bonds which link me to the past. I must forge these bonds because the past is present to me. It lives in my presence and I need to determine how it will dwell within me. The past world is my present, my existence is determined in it, but I depend upon the word, the visions and the dreams which come to me in the desert of my soul. There I find my images and metaphors, my tones and transfigurations. The I discovers what it means when it says: "I think therefore I am." In the desert I form my commentaries to the "I think." Descartes might not have understood the I as commentary, but he would have grasped my intent and looked upon me with understanding. He

---

[3]Ibid., 163.

did not know what it meant to wander in the desert, to be a child of exile, a nomadic wanderer. I understand how he avoided this experience, and dwelt in splendid isolation. The past gave me my destiny and I had to live with it. I lived with exile because my people dwelled alone in the universe. They lived as strangers with their neighbors. They were a backward-looking people.

"Between the word heard and the word to be said, in this half silence which is the last refuge of the echo, there is my place."[4] The poet showed us the meaning of place. Place is essential to understanding and to the imagination. Without place, we lose our capacity to see reality. Place determines our ability to embrace, to grasp the reality about us, but of even greater significance, place allows us to be receptive, to hear. Seeing is possible because we have been taught to see, hearing is possible because we have learned to listen. We have acquired or conquered place. We know how to see and how to hear. Jabès stated that between "the word heard and the word said" we search for place. Place is the "between," the incomprehensible "somewhere" which makes it possible for us to listen and to see. We have heard and we have seen. There is no seeing nor listening without the primordial hearing and seeing of the word. The words turn upon themselves. They reveal those precious nuances which allow us to understand the place of man, the meaning of place in man's attempt to approach reality. More than hearing and obeying is hearing and listening. Learning to listen is the destiny of life, listening to what is being said, listening through my hearing, piercing the words for the words that live behind them, knowing that in everything that appears and is heard there is a world that has not appeared and has not been heard. Through the negation of the immediate world, we enter another. "A word," Jabès noted, "is tiny in its scope of revelation, immense in the scantiness of the sign. The book is always open."[5] The wonder of the word is that it is revelatory. We must discover the faintness of the signs it hears within itself. Each man reads the signs differently, his perception and intuitive capacity is distinct. We live with these subtle nuances and find in them the complexities of his experience. Each man seeks the desert, the place of images, of forms, and of the formless.

In the desert, the formlessness of forms makes us realize the scantiness of the signs. The desert is the place of their contemplation. "My work," the poet said, "is a book of sand, not only in its light, but in its stark nakedness."[6] The poet reveals the truth of a vision: the book is

---

[4]Ibid., 164.
[5]Ibid.
[6]Ibid.

being written from and in the sands. The book is a nomadic text, born again and again from exilic wandering which returns to the desert and draws its images and dreams from the shifting sands. In the desert, being and nonbeing are wedded like life and death. The desert lets us see images which will remain only for the fleeting moment, which will bring forth others. Things pass away as others are born. Over and over again, the meaning of the phoenix comes before us. We become attuned to the coming into being and the passing away of reality. We feel the delicacy that is inherent in human creativity, the precariousness of its nature and the rarity of its emergence. We think of the "book of sand" growing and changing from image to image. The book dies in fixity, and is alive in the sands of the desert. There it grows with its images and visions, there it defies man's attempt to absolutize the word, to give it a final and absolute form. The book is the negation of this form. The "book of sand" is the abyss of nothingness, the labyrinth in which forms find their demise. The writer lives and moves in devotion to the book. He is a writer because the book is his light. He lives from the formless forms which is the book. He writes because he needs to transfigure and transform reality. The pen is the instrument of change and metamorphosis. The writer is the believer in the word behind the word, in the book behind the books. The writer defies the immediate, the appearing. He listens to the purity of the poetic word.

We listen to words which reveal strikingly the fabric of the human experience. "You can love," Jabès said, "only what you can destroy or what daily destroys you. Such is the love of God."[7] How painfully contradictory and startling are these words. They attract and fascinate us because they pierce our attitudes and shatter our stability. If we think of the validity of this love, if we realize that if it were man's love, it would destroy the fabric of humankind, we would know why the love of God and the love of man are so radically separated from each other. The more man longs to approach God, the more revealing and visible is the abysmal separation. This separation shows how contradictory is every human expression about God. From our place in the universe, God is contradiction. He is the death of man as man is the death of God. Human love is creative and destructive; divine love contradictory and devastating. Divine love is human demise. God's mercy lies in his distance from man; the greater the separation, the greater the mercy. Man longs to approach God, to seek his love and mercy. The deeper the search, the more intense the longing, the greater the transfiguration of the divine into the idol of the imagination. Man's love of God has meaning only in his relationship to his fellowman. The death of God, his

[7]Ibid.

absence in our presence, is man's salvation. We wander in exile because there has been no redemption. The Messiah remains beyond time and space as we remain and grow within these forms. Man's redemption ends the history of man, ends the quality of human history, the sense of becoming which is its reality. God's mercy toward man lies in his death. God dies in order that man lives. This is the supreme moment of religious life, the metamorphosis of God's death into the depths of human existence.

When we leave the common places of our existence, we become aware that there are possibilities we have never probed. The world can appear so differently to those of us who change place and learn how to listen and to see. What appears before us is the opening to realities we have not yet seen. The door is open waiting for us to enter, but we rarely walk in. The ghosts of powerful and ugly guards frighten us; we wait, grow old, and die. We have never entered. The images are Kafka's and they remind us of the realities we will never see nor hear. We will never enter the door open to us. Only the poet dares to enter, to walk through the gigantic figures which block the way, images of defiance, visions of man's weaknesses and subjugation. Kafka expressed the need to be awakened, startled, and shocked if we were to shake off the lethargy which dominates our existence. In a letter to his friend Oscar Pollak, dated January 27, 1904, he wrote: "I believe that we should read only those books that bite and sting us. If a book we are reading does not arouse us with a blow to the head, then why read it?... What we need are books that affect us like some really grievous misfortune, like the death of one whom we loved more than ourselves, as if we were banished to distant forests, away from everybody, like a suicide, a book must be the ax for the frozen sea within us. That is what I believe."[8]

The image of the ax and the frozen sea makes us realize how each being goes into exile, becomes a nomadic wanderer. We must be able to begin the endless journey through life which leaves every dwelling in search of a new land. The book, like the desert, is the ax which tears down what we have built and revered. We open the seas, to release the invisible and the unknown, to return us to the visions and dreams which form human life. Kafka reveals the image of that dance of life and death which is life. The artist is always breaking out of the cage, which is always in search of him. We learn to escape the cage, to wander in the desert with "the book of sands." Where there is nowhere to halt, no place of refuge, there is no concealment. The people of the book have learned the meaning of exile, dwelling where there is no dwelling, yearning for the book which is beyond all books, for promise where there are only

---

[8]F. Kafka, *Autobiographical Writings*, (New York: Schocken Books, 1974) 7.

hopes and dreams. Jabès wrote the odyssey of exile, which is the fate of those who contemplate humankind. The poets of exile are nomads. We long to give them permanent places in our museums, but they defy our definitions and discontentment. They live in fear.

In the exile we hear the cries of those who ask about their being, who exclaim again and again: Who am I? The poet wanders alone, in painful and stubborn solitude, moving from image to image, finding in neither one nor the other a dwelling which gives us place and rest. The search for recognition is endless. We look into the eyes of others to find the love which we seek, but in our wanderings these eyes are rare, and we turn to ourselves asking again about the meaning of our existence. In a world where we are nomads, few take us in. We move differently and strangely; the others regard us suspiciously from their door steps, and we know that we are unwanted and so remain alone. "The poet speaks of stars, myriads of pierced eyes. A blind universe sees God."[9] Our solitude makes us sensitive to the blindness about us, to a universe which in its blindness sees God. Those who see through their seeing, who listen to their hearing, know that God died with the creation. We only know that his presence is his absence, his truth is his concealment. For the wanderer, there are only the images of a concealed God, the obscurity of the abyss, the God who is a labyrinth.

"The adventure of looking (mutual need to see and be seen)," Jabès said, "leads man into a confounding examination of himself and the world, each depending upon the other, each annulled through the other in confessed impotence and hunger which writing on the bottom of the abyss takes on with its last bit of strength."[10] Nothing strikes us more fundamentally and deeply than the realization of the separability of all things. Consciously things don't belong to each other, nor does the self belong to the self. We are aware of an unbridgeable separation between things that exist. We live in a world that has lost its order, which has to be put together again through the word we impose upon it. We are sure of only one thing: the inseparability which accompanies what we think and what we do. This indisputable point, this place from which we think and imagine, is the link between man and man, between man and the world. The exile of the spirit bears witness to this inseparability which is overcome only in the book, in the words we string together, but which later fade away. Writing struggles to hold together an order that is disorder, an image which will yield images. This is the nomadic journey, the movement from image to image, from place to place. The more we examine ourselves, the more we become conscious of how different and

---

[9]"Elya," 166.
[10]Ibid., 166.

alone we are from what is supposed to belong to us. Solitude is the realization of those who have accepted the exilic world, who are the creatures of the desert, who bare the fate of restlessness and dissatisfaction.

"My books," Jabès said, "testify to the impossible approach of His name. I have lived at an immense distance from the Kingdom I often thought I had reached."[11] The vastness of the distance between God and the self frightens the soul. We wonder if such a distance can be overcome, if we don't find in writing what others have found in tradition and retreat, if for those who have no roots there is only the force of the pen. What others find in the book of prayer, the writer finds in the book of images; what the writer brings forth in forms and images, the believer has already learned to repeat from the Teaching. The believer finds inspiration and comfort in the truths of the Fathers; he has his place, and is joyful in his dwelling. The writer has forsaken this dwelling. He is indifferent to this tradition, but also inspired by it. He accepts its existence, but needs to go beyond it. He needs to create where the believer accepts. He needs to be spontaneous, in addition to his sensitivity to receptivity. Neither spontaneity nor receptivity are enough. In one, he discovers the exaggerated enthusiasm of the creative I. In the other, he feels the captivity of the receptive world. In neither reality can the poet survive. He journeys *between* them, balancing one with the other. In Jabès, we find the beauty of balance. His wanderings are those of Jewish existence. They reveal the spirituality of an exile which is a fate, an inescapable odyssey. This is a fate which is shared with all men who walk fearlessly in an unending journey with the absent God, opening to every traveler a communication between self and the absence of presence. The believer knows no more than the writer; each has learned to respond differently to the presence of the desert in the self and to the exile of the generations.

"If He did not exist," Jabès wrote, "I would have howled to His glory. I despise those who see Him, because they only look on themselves. He is the invisible seer of our invisible world. O to make ourselves seeing to become His equals in nothingness."[12] We chase God from our lives to realize self-domination and autonomy. We call upon him in the presence of his absence. These are the movements of human existence defying captivity in one direction, and exaggeration in the other. Where are we between God's presence and his absence? We are Jews. We have no permanent domicile. We are in exile from every dwelling, defiant of every fixed image. Spiritual life begins in wandering,

---

[11]Ibid., 167.
[12]Ibid.

leaving the home and going toward the new land. Leaving is beginning, denying what *is*, to bring forth what is yet to be. "I despise those who see Him" are the words of freedom and negation. They are the words of violence which shake the foundation of given and believed truths. These must be questioned and fought. Nothing in human existence escapes the violence of the question. Where this violence is absent, there thinking has become confession and acceptance. God is neither here nor there. He is nothingness, the invisible. We do not love a God who is present. Familiarity destroys such love. We have tried to form dialogues with him, create those amorous I-Thou relationships which transfigure God into a lover, satisfying our need to be loved and to love. But the divine escapes this desire for equality. He escapes into the abysmal reality which is divinity. The equality we seek are the words written in the abyss. The glory of man lies in the labyrinth of God's being, in the unknown and unreal which are his expressions. The absence of being lies at the source of man's being. In the awareness of this absence, man discovers traces of divinity.

God dies in our thought of his existence. It is our thinking which is his demise. Why, we ask, does he die in our thoughts if we know that we cannot avoid thinking of him? We only know that the more we bring him into our thinking, the more we have made him into our image. In our thinking, we worship the God of our being, the God who is no longer God but the self. "You did not die, Lord, of having been, but of having thought you were."[13] Man likewise dies in the thought of his being. It is this being which man must leave before he goes into exile. Human life is the escape from being, the struggle to leave the place of being which has tied us land and people. Spiritually, we belong only to the commentaries and discussions we have created through the generations. The death of our self-consciousness is the beginning of our wanderings, of opening ourselves to what is yet to be. Awareness affirms the presence of being. This awareness must dissolve into a negation of self-consciousness. This negation is the start of our travels, the opening to a world which lies behind the appearances of being, a world created through metamorphosis. The search of the writer is in the powers of transfiguration and transformation. In these lie the divinity alive in human existence. Writing is driven by the love of the invisible, of the book from which books emerge, the book of books, the sacred light in which light becomes light. "Turning to the book," Jabès remarked, "must mean having guessed that we metamorphose in the word, that in it we promptly die."[14] Death in the word is our life. We are released from a

---

[13]Ibid., 168.
[14]Ibid.

stage of reality and driven toward another. Death is the creative power of nonbeing, of that absence in and from which everything takes life.

Consciousness freed from being is the violence of nonbeing, the silence in which we find God. Nonbeing is the distance separating consciousness from the object of perception. In nonbeing, consciousness finds a reality of its own, an independent and autonomous reality, the realm of pure poetry. In this realm the mind thinks upon itself, creating images from its images, dreams from its dreams. How do we comprehend this realm of pure poetry? We do not. We experience it in our struggle to be beyond the realm of sense perception, to find in the mind the realm of creativity. We lose our dependence upon the senses when we realize that thinking is thinking upon self. We are not dependent upon what we see or hear in order to comprehend how we form and develop ideas and images. The poet taught us to roam the sands of the desert in search of images. He showed us the exile from the senses, the nomadic wanderings of the imagination, the nonbeing which lives in being and the violence which shatters our forms, enabling us to build new ones. The poet enhanced reality to the creativity of the spirit. He raised reality to the realm of creativity. The greatness of man belongs to this power of transformation. No other being transfigures what he perceives. Man alone carries the experience of the spirit with him from generation to generation, leaving the legacy of commentary to those whose receptivity allows them to receive it. The death of the commentators is their life in the present. Death and life create the movements of the spirit, appearing again and again to us like the moments of the phoenix. The ashes of one generation bear within them the life of the next, who are awaiting to be awakened in the minds of those whose spirit is their domicile.

Jabès wrote the odyssey of the poetic response. His poetry and prose embrace Israel's legacy of commentaries, of books of teachings, of meditations on the book of books. In the depths of despair and doubt, of absence and obscurity, Israel remained stubborn and loyal to the book. In God's absence, the poet found his presence; in the desert the poet sought the endless images and dreams which exile brought with it. The poet was the exilic wanderer, listening to the words of the book, hearing the endless attempt of the people responding to their fate. He heard and he responded. He wrote an epic, one that has no beginning and no end, one that belongs to the perpetual drama of trust and doubt, of life and death. Never before has a poet attempted such a mosaic. Never before has a poetry of response been so comprehensive in its lack of comprehensiveness. So much is left to the reader, so much whiteness is left to him to write his own responses, to join with the poet in the commentaries that have been written from generation to generation. In his despair, the poet never yielded to anarchy, nor to the deification of pure poetry. The poet remained a nomad with his God. He always looked upward to the stars, to those bits of whiteness in the blackness of the heavens. There he saw hints of the divine encompassed in darkness, as life was encompassed in death. The poet was the child of the desert. The desert was his domicile, but like the fleeting sands, the domicile had no form nor order. It grew and faded away, it was life and death coming into being and passing away. Here lived the solitude which came with the book that was always being written and fading away. This was not a chosen solitude, but a metaphysical one. This was solitude over which man has no dominance. It is the solitude of exile, of being and nonbeing, of God's absence in God's presence. Man, like the sands, fades into one form to be born into another. He knows only that the desert is there and will always be there, like the book which is there and cannot be grasped and controlled. The poet lived in exile and in the book. He turned away from chaos and exaggerated self-importance. He was always a commentator. He was the poet of commentary. He wrote the epic of commentary.

Speaking of the book, the poet said:

> The dark has the light for its past, and the light the dark.
>
> Whichever path we take, the past sputters in the distance like the bit of a wick.
>
> We find the candle where we left it for the time of a reading.
>
> The book is the place of these far-flung comings and goings.
>
> ---from night to night, from this side of the past to the other.[15]

All things take place within the book. The book hovers over our existence like an embracing truth which we long to approach but which is always beyond our grasp. Like the sands in our hands, and the vapors of the dew, we reach out to seize it and it evades our fingers, flees from our chase. The vapors are present, reminding us of their existence, telling us that they are not our children. They belong to us only as realities which make us aware of our finiteness. We live with forces we do not control. We move through the desert, see the images of our visions, the dreams of formless forms, and we discover that we are children of fate. The desert is not an external reality; it is within us. The desert is our fate. "The work I write," Jabès said, "immediately rewrites itself in the book. This repeatability is part of its own breathing and the reduplication of each of its signs."[16]

15Ibid., 323.
16Ibid.

We are fascinated by the rewriting of the book. Here we touch upon the deepest experience of Israel: the incessant rewriting of the book, the cyclical reading of the book, the never-ending repetition and reduplication of the text. But repetition is always accomplished with a new tone and an unexpected nuance. The poet wanders with the book, knowing that it absorbs into itself all books, and is their source. The book breathes the tones and nuances of repetition, the cycle of exilic wanderings which has no fixed beginning and no determined end. But the book is the beginning and the end. It hovers over human reality like the vastness of the seas and the heavens. The poet spoke of repeatability to reveal the infinite dimensions of the book from which everything proceeds and to which everything returns. In the book, nothing is new. The book is nothingness, the source of being and nonbeing. Neither being nor nonbeing have reality apart from the book. The world is not determined by the conflict of being and nonbeing. The world has its source in nothingness which precedes being, is the eternal *Before*, the word we hear when we speak of being and nonbeing, the word of the abyss. Jabès is the poet of the abyss. Never does he find his dwelling in a fixed series of oppositions and contradictions. His realm surpasses their contradictions. He lives in the unknowable and indeterminable. Jabès wandered with us into the realm of the labyrinth. He revealed the incomprehensible divinity which would never approach the realm of being, whose distance was sacred, piercing, and dominating. Jabès journeyed this sacred distance in the desert with the book.

Jabès spoke always of the book. He spoke of a book that had no place, a book which covered all existence, which embraced the deserts and the seas, the heavens and the lands, the book which was everywhere and nowhere. He said:

> The book is my home. It has always been the home of my words
>
> You lived by words which were stolen again and again. My words are this home.
>
> Then I won't have any words?
>
> Then I won't have any home?[17]

The book is the dwelling which is always being taken from us. Its words are taken by others to create dwellings which are foreign to us. The words are taken from us by those who want to possess them. We are deprived of our dwelling. We take the words from each other. We send our neighbors away without words. We appropriate them solely for ourselves. We go into exile with our words, to save them from those who

---

[17]Ibid., 273.

want to give them permanency, who gather them into a single dwelling. For them *the* book has become *a* book. It has found a place, but the book has no place. It is the creator of place and does not occupy a place. Where the book has become *a* book, the poet no longer sees it nor can he hear its words. They have become ritualistic chants and articles of faith. They have found dwellings, and are chiseled in stone. Men come to learn their sounds, to repeat them to their children from generation to generation. The words have died in the repetition. They no longer belong to the spirit. Men paint them on their banners, create songs with them, and force others to repeat the same words. The poet no longer has a home. He no longer has words. Deprived of them, he wanders the earth as a madman, crying for the words and the home he no longer possesses. He cries for the words which have become stones for their possessor who has deprived them of their exile. The madman is crying for the redemption of the word.

The poet faces madness. He faces the madness of words engraved in stone, words which are no longer wanderers, words which no longer reveal the desert in them. For Jabès, being Jewish meant being in the desert. He stated that for him "being Jewish means therefore, being at the heart of an essential interrogation. Called into question by the heirs of his questions, his certainties glow under the ashes. For everyday is a day of ordeals. Stirring the ashes, how many hours do we awaken that were never seized.... Even more than by his speech the Jew is a Jew by the silence or the vast murmur which encloses his eyes as a sea surrounds an island and makes it inaccessible."[18]

This interrogation creates the poetic verse and prose which form this spiritual odyssey. Its endless wandering defies the imagination, and is a stumbling block for reason, which for one reason or another wants the interrogation to end. We like the taste of the answer, the sweetness of the conclusion which gives us rest. The poet offered no such tranquillity. The exile, the nomadic life has no end. It is the defiance of such tranquillity. It refuses to be embodied in the stone of death; it refuses to become an article of faith. It resists becoming a religious instrument. It holds up a no to every attempt to embrace it within a religious form. The poet struggled for his exilic life. He struggled for the freedom of the word. He knew that only the word was sacred in its exile. The profane emerges from its permanency, its ritualistic embodiment.

With sublime clarity, Jabès observed: "The desert wrote the Jew, and the Jew reads himself in the desert."[19] The desert is an island, a refuge of images and dreams. Along its limits are the cities where people study the

---

[18]Ibid., 299.
[19]Ibid., 302.

book which emerged from the desert. For them it is a history which they teach to their children, a memory which they preserve in their homes, churches, and synagogues. This is the memory from which the people emerge, and from which they recognize each other in the world. The poet needed more than memories, narratives, and history. He knew of "exile within the essence of ties," he knew that this exile within the ties was their essence. The exile of the desert is the exile embodied in the forms created by the desert. The desert tied the people to a past, but the tie did not give them permanency, it did not provide the dwelling of tranquillity which they sought from its experience. The desert created the eternal wanderers, the endless interrogation, and the fleeting dwellings for a people condemned to be alone. Beyond the Law, the ceremonies and rituals which are the dwellings of the Jews, Jabès found another realm, the drama of Jewish existence, the rupture between God and man, the rupture which conditions the word, and leaves it to the realm of man. In man's word, we experience the absence of God and the attempt to form Jewish existence from this absence of both God and his world. Man builds the word as metaphor and metonymy. He discovers the mystery of its nuances and tonality. He finds the mystery of its colors. This is his response to the rupture, which he finds in the word.

From the negation of the word comes the name. The word has died as the divine word; it comes forth as the exilic word. It is the name of the wanderer who comes from the desert to the city, and begins to tell us of the odyssey of the man who found the God of absence, who discovered rupture, and roamed the face of the earth, relating his story of solitude and faith. He tells the story of the book which is always being written, which has no beginning and no end. This is the sacred book which never leaves the wanderer, it is always with him. It is the book from which he writes his books. It is the book of poetry from which poetry comes forth and to which it returns. Jabès shows us the way to exile, the way to life, which is the way of exile. He shows us the way of the wanderer, the man who belongs to everything and belongs to nothing. Jabès is the poetic wanderer. He is the poet of the word which is also in exile, the word which has become nomadic, the word of solitude, the word that has lost the word. There is a profound mystery in Jabès's odyssey. We read, we write, we reread, we rewrite.

9

The Crushing Reality of Divinity in Man

At the beginning of *El, or The Last Book,* Jabès quotes an aphorism from Franz Kafka: "It is up to us to accomplish the negative. The positive is given."[1] The positive is our fate. It is that first experience which we confront, although it is not the first experience which we know. "The positive is given." These words strike as a revelation which reveals our finiteness, the fleeting quality of time and space. We face our habits and our traditions and they become strange, worn out, indefensible. They tire us. They are our traditions. We have rarely questioned them. We learned to hear and repeat them and put them easily aside. Often we are told to listen to the wonders they embody, to the melodies and enchantments they yield. How strikingly unique, we are told, they are! We listen and we become accustomed to their tones. We hear melodic beauty in them. The positive is given in many ways, but what we realize is that we are always passive in our acceptance, that we need conformity, and are satisfied with its pleasures and tastes. But we are never fully at peace. There are realities yet to be born, which don't yield to conformity and acceptance. Realities have occurred politically and spiritually which we have not yet seen nor heard. We are always behind the events, catching up to their existence. We are always behind the events, not aware that their negation is the beginning of their reality. We feel, and slowly begin to know, that reality begins in its absence, in the violence of negation. In this violence which accompanies negation, we discover the source of our spirituality, the labyrinth of our creativity. We are men because we are the power of negation, because we say no to the yes and yes to the no. In the negating word lies man's unfathomable mystery, the need to explore

---

[1]*The Book of Questions, El, or The Last Book,* vol. VII (Middletown: Wesleyan University Press, 1984), 6.

the forces dwelling in negation. Man discovers that the burst of energy which is the beginning of creation is the no to the given. This is not a discovery which man makes by himself. This is a reality which the positive in its changeless forms imposes upon him. The positive calls forth his psychological and metaphysical dissatisfaction.

We speak of this relationship of negation as the point of divinity dwelling within the creation. It is the crushing power of divinity dwelling in man. At this point creation loses its autonomy, it is no longer absolute. It can be changed, transformed, and transfigured. "Unimaginable encounter," Jabès remarked, "of what is on the point of becoming with what is about to be dispersed again. The tried word blossoms in an ordeal where it is both hangman and victim."[2] At this point, all things lose their independence. We discover the metaphorical reality of human creativity. The world is not simply given and perceived; it is reformed and developed. The human journey began at the moment when man realized that reality is not unidimensional, that a multiplicity of worlds exists, unending in physical and spiritual possibilities. It is the presence of the book in which the endless is being written endlessly. It is the book of sands forever moving in one direction and then in another. The poet is our guide through the labyrinth of these movements. With him we become explorers of the word. He learned the powers of the word, the reality of wandering, and the meaning of exile. The poet is the exilic wanderer. We learn from him how to wander, how to comprehend the word. Above all, we learn about the book. The book we cannot read. It is the source of all books, the book which is alive but is not personal, the book which we love, which remains invisible and beyond our thinking. The presence of the book is its power, and from this power all things take their movement. In a theoretical way it is an "unmoved mover." The book preserves us from anarchy, from the terror of unrestrained subjectivity. The book forces us to know that in its presence all human thought has its point, the point of mystery, the point of beginning, the origin of being.

The desert is always present in us and we return to it again and again, attempting to discover the undiscoverable, to find the formless forms of the imagination. In the shifting dunes of the desert we lay aside the absolute which man loves passionately. We lay aside its security, and the falsity of its promises. The absolute becomes a dune among dunes, a fleeting form or mirage which distorts our judgment. In the desert, we experience the power and helplessness of the word. We find its pervasive inadequacy, but in this inadequacy we grasp its strength. The inadequacy becomes the force of man's endeavor to fathom the meaning

---

[2]Ibid., 4.

of the word. The great struggle of human existence is the fight to enhance the word, to explore the analogy and the metaphor. With the word, man becomes a creator of reality, a source of forms. In this same creator lives the death of the word. In him the word is not only born, but dies. The word loses its divine source. It lies in human finiteness covered with inadequacy and exaggerated pride. Truth and the word are brought together in an unidentifiable identification. Man searches for the divine word in the human, and he creates idolic monstrosities. "The desert," the poet said, "is a space where one step gives way to the next, which undoes it, and the horizon means hope for a tomorrow which speaks, where the pact is the point."[3]

The desert reveals our finitude. It is a place which denies the absolute quality of place as it denies the fleeting quality of time from within time. Philosophers and poets have turned us from the heavens, from the whiteness of the stars, to the inevitable laws governing the geography which surrounds us. We look for salvation in the cyclical changes of the seasons, the identification between nature and human life, a range of satisfying changes and developments of human life. Man, the earth, the home, work, and necessity create a romantic blend of blood and soil which puts aside the exile of Abraham and his tribe. In these attachments and devotions, the exile is lost, the nomadic life is tailored to the earth. The divine is now the identification of man and soil, of place and labor, of necessity and change. The book is dead. It is the silent cry of the believer. The book is buried in the soil which is mixed with labor and sweat. The book has found a material dwelling. It is written in the changes of the seasons, in the "holiness" of the soil which man holds as sacred matter. All is revealed in this sacred relationship of man and soil: love of country, of people, and of tradition. The book cries out from its burial. It is not the soil nor the work, nor the laws of nature, the heat, the cold, the rain, the snow. The book is the concealment of the invisible, the light in the darkness. The book is written by and in the exile and its wanderers. The book is the *yet to be* in opposition to the *now*. It recorded the demise of God in his creation, and man's powers of the negation. It revealed the presence and reality of the divine absence. It moves man away from the positive. It shows him the reality of absence, in which the spiritual reveals the qualitative meaning of the beginning, that leap of the spirit into the unknown, the source of reality.

In solitude, the creator identified his word. Alone among the moving dunes the word is heard and listened to. There it is born, because there it dies. There it discovers its strength and frailty; there it finds exile. The word is hidden among men. It becomes a nomadic wanderer in search of

---

[3]Ibid.

a dwelling. The man who listens and goes toward it wants to guard and preserve it, but the word dies. It longs for the vastness of the sea, the light, and darkness of the heavens. Its soil is negation. It finds life and nourishment in it. It defies the positive, and the permanent.

"A point so small, and yet it holds the ashes of all other points."[4] We must imagine such a point where all others find their demise and their life. This is the point we call God: the smallest which is the largest, and the greatest which is sublime, and invisible. The point is God, but it is where God is always becoming God. God is always moving from, and to, the point. The point is the death and the rebirth of God. The world is reborn at the point because it is at the point that the world dies. Everything is related to the point, yet nothing is the reality of the point. Into this nothing, all reality flows. The impermanency of being emerges from its relationship to the nothingness of the point. Hovering over being is this impermanency. The positive does not grow only from its being, but also from its negation. Hovering over being is its demise and its rebirth, its coming into being and its passing away. The wandering through being is a travel through the changing metamorphosis of human life. We see beyond our seeing. We listen, and we hear beyond our listening. Realms of unknown reality form the fabric of the world. Existence is incomplete and disordered. Man builds with disorder. He destroys and brings with him order. The interplay of order and disorder affects our senses, causes them to acknowledge the metaphoric reality of man's spirit. We are the point of human life, but in us violence and reason form the bases of our creation, the point of the movement from life to death and from death to life. In a diminutive way, man and God have similarities and we, at times, can speak of analogies, but these fade quickly, and the chaos which afflicts human existence submerges the creativity from which it seeks redemption.

"Yesterday and tomorrow," Jabès remarked, "are halves of one and the same point." The movement from yesterday to tomorrow has no given path. The signs are not clear. The direction can hardly be seen, but we see through the mist with a light that forces us to link yesterday with tomorrow. We can speak of a "dialectic of seeing." We see through what appears to us. We see in bold and clear reality what is appearing to us. If we believe that reality lies in what is before us, then our seeing is constantly and persistently observing the details, the forms, the relationships of what is given to us by man's activities and productions. What is significant is what man does and how he does it. The doing embodies his values. Doing and valuing are one. If the "dialectic of seeing" shows us how to pass through perception, to see images in

---

[4]Ibid.

images, visions in visions, we hesitantly, but continually, approach the realm of the imagination. This is the realm in which the meanings and powers of the I think emerge in their fullest. Seeing frees us to enter the realm of the immediacies of impressions exploring with a constancy their implications and significance. It makes it possible for us to transfigure and metamorphosize our impressions, to reveal them as metaphors, analogies, and symbols. With these rhetorical instruments, whose capacities we discover only in using them, we find realms of being which are unknown and concealed. This concealment, and the veils which embrace them, are the hidden doors through which man enters, but which he finds profoundly difficult to penetrate. We wonder how it is possible to see through the doors of being fiercely guarded by tradition and habit. These hound us like guardsmen. They shatter man's imaginary powers. Yesterday and tomorrow look alike. They belong to each other because we see them so often together. But they are antagonists, each in search of its reality, separating its realm from the other to justify its independence and autonomy. They are friends dependent upon each other, finding in each other nourishment and awareness.

We are moved from one position to another. We have little time to rest in one before we are called forth by the other. We can't prevent our seeing and listening from wandering beyond one place to look at another, in order to find what is different and to explore it. We are wanderers, nomads of the soul finding satisfaction nowhere, but searching everywhere. The wandering images carry us from realm to realm, from being to being, from negation to negation. Writing is our exile; we explore, examine, follow one path after another, leave one to travel on another, never forgetting the first, wondering where it would have taken us, and longing to return and satisfy our wonder. Rarely can we remain on one path without uneasiness and pain. Nomads we were, nomads we remain.

"Love is death's crystal day, oblivion its opaque night."[5] Love is in love with love, but love is always escaping love, seeking more than the love which it loves. Love embraces death. Death embraces love. Nothing is more forceful in love than absence and negation. Love is birth, and birth is death. The more we realize how closely dependent love and death are upon each other, the more we realize that it is only in love that death discovers the power of its negation, only in the surge for life does death become more visible. Love is that unconquerable movement toward form. Looming over this urge is the reality of death, clear and sharp in its striking capacity to give strength and longing to life. Life

---

[5]Ibid., 7.

longs to perpetuate its movement, to expand its capacities. Losing this capacity, it dims the clarity of death. It deprives it of negation, of the absence which is its substance. Writing tells the story of this embrace of life and death. Writing tells about this relationship which embraces humankind. Dependence fills the book. It is the object of our love. It dies and lives in its death, as God is alive in his absence. We are embraced by the death of divinity. This is the concealment and oblivion in which we move through the world. The death of God is not an escape from him. It is a bond from which we have no freedom. We have only a fate and a destiny. We proclaim the concealment of God whose presence hovers over us. In every creation death appears in life. Life without God has no meaning, but it is life in whose reality God is absence. This absence deprives life of its divinity, but gives it its humanity. This is the mystery of human life, which is real only because God died. Wandering with the poet, seeing and hearing echoes of the embrace between life and death, we become more and more sensitive to the precariousness of life. We wander with a saddened joy through the realms of being, attempting to comprehend this movement of life toward death and death toward life. "How beautiful you are Sarah, lying here, naked, while I looked for you wherever you are not, where you no longer are, wrote Yukel."[6]

The love of the book is the inclusive experience of Israel. But the book is invisible. Our eyes have lost their physical vision of the book. The book has become like the seas and the desert; it has become unfathomable, complete in its incompleteness, written and unwritten. The book lives but has died, and from its death it has emerged as the book of life and death. The book belongs to humanity in exile from its dwelling, searching for a universe which is incomplete, but imaginable to those who ponder its reality. The universe is a dwelling which has never become a dwelling, a voice that is both heard and silent. No matter where we search for the universe, whether in the material world or in the desert, we find that gentle embrace between absence and presence.

The poet noted that "the sage dipped his reed pen into the inkwell, pulled it out, and held it for a few moments, as if in doubt, above the page where he had not yet noted anything that day. Then, to his pupil's surprise, he drew a small circle in a corner of the blotter he always kept within reach. The circle, he said, which the blotter has made into a point invaded by night, is God. Why did you want the circle to turn into a black point? And why should this stain among so many others on your blotter be God? the disciple asked."[7] All questions about God have a mystery hovering over them. The mystery lies in the human question

---

[6]Ibid.
[7]Ibid., 7-8.

attempting to point to God. But the attempt is unsure and obscure. God could be a black point, the moving dunes of the desert, the never-ending waves of the seas, the stars in the heavens. No matter if he is a point, a wave, a flow of sand, he is the unknown who dies as we approach, who emerges in the distance as an utterance, a word, a sound, a calling. Man probes with his words what cannot be probed. Man questions what cannot be questioned, and what is always questioned. Easily man interrogates what he perceives, and in this interrogation he seeks to separate truth from falsehood. This is the source of knowledge, of the technological advances upon which humankind depends. There is the other dimension where the questions float into the labyrinth of being, where the visible fades into the invisible, and what looms before us is the majesty of the stars, the points of light which mirror the light in its resplendent beauty. In the infinitesimal point, the light intensity is at its greatest. In the infinitesimally small lies the creation, the origin of the beginning, the nothingness from which form emerges. The sage with his small circle allowed us a glimpse at divinity.

"God refused image and language in order to be Himself the point. He is image in the absence of images, language in the absence of language, point in the absence of points." God's refusal is the preservation of language. Language is man's creation, the preserve of his imagination and thinking. God's withdrawal is man's agony and his freedom. God's silence is man's voice. "Vowels make us see, make us hear. Vowels are image and song. In our ancestor's script vowels are points."[8] God withdrew from images to be image in the absence of the image. God withdraws from the world in order that the world belong to man, that it become his creation, the work of his hands and his productivity. God's withdrawal is the source of man's painful creativity, his search for divinity and freedom. Where God dwells, man finds no dwelling. Where man hears God's word, he loses his language. Where the divine image is present, man fears and trembles. God has no image, no language. He redeems man in his refusal to speak, to be present in a law or a dwelling. Man sings to God his praise because he can only praise and love God in the reality of God's absence. What is present comes to be destruction, what is absent is the source of redemption. Man loves only what is invisible, the reality of his misery and his persistence.

Nothing shines more brightly in the universe of the poet than the startling brilliancy of negation and absence. These are the stars which guided the poet and led him through the darkness of the heavens. They brought him to the book, to the wonders of the desert and the vastness of the seas. Jabès created an odyssey in and through which he transfigured

---

[8]Ibid., 15.

the world. He filled it with metaphors, signs, symbols, analogies, and metonymies. He recreated the world in the image of the exile of Israel, of the moving dunes of the desert, and of the present and the absent book. The odyssey of the exilic wanderer became the metaphor of all wanderings which emerged from this exilic image. Language wanders with the metaphors and their dwellings. Not even God is fixed in his absence, or in his withdrawal. In the wanderings of the poet, images flow from images. There is no goal; there is only the experience of the journey, the unexpected and the unknown. We go forward to the land which is yet to be, which we see and hear metaphorically. The land is always *away from here*. It is the other of what we see and hear. It will always be the other. Men find lands and languages, build homes and form nations, give allegiance to governments and struggle to bolster their loyalties. The exilic people are loyal to land but also to the landless, to the historical voice, and also to the voice of silence. The people are embraced in the book which is over and around them, and in which they have found their fate. They are in love with the book which is the source of all books, the book which is read in silence, with parables and paradoxes.

"No trace of blood," Jabès remarked, "remains where I have passed. What could be more natural? Only absence has the power to endure, but its oblivion shapes the negation into a dazzling point, a sun beyond alliance, beyond allegiance, beyond eternity."[9] Again and again we hear the words which tell us that "only absence has the power to endure," that our world is created from the powers of negation, from the exile of the word, from the withdrawal of God from his creation. Absence creates worlds of uncertainty and inadequacy. These are the worlds in which man creates his arts and sciences, in which he discovers the I think and I do, the origins of his humanity, the converting fires of his spirituality which deny him permanency and adaptation. Absence is man's liberation from the conditions in which he finds his natural existence. Man denies nature. The world was created in reference to man, and, if this is his assumption, then man struggles against nature. Nature guards the privileges of the animals and insects; it is the reality which man changes and recreates.

Negation is the "dazzling point" of man's humanity. The violence of negation is the origin of his reason and imagination. Freed from the presence of God, man finds in his absence the negation and the vitality of man's own life. This vitality ennobles and destroys him. Man discovers that negation is his greatest creative destructive force. How ignoble is his nobility in science and art when his quest for truth is distorted by his deification of his capacity for autonomy. Man is alone in the world with

---

[9]bid., 9.

negative powers; God released in him a force of unimaginable brutality. Man's demise is a reality. There is only the remembrance of the solitude and sufferings of the book, of the desert, and the agony of the exilic wandering. These reduce man to his finiteness, and dim his glory. Man rediscovers the reality of his limitation.

Jabès observed: "You had to learn to deserve your truth. The Jews know that it is not enough to believe in a truth, that we must, each time, deserve it. There is no merit but in the stubborn effort to reach it. Does stating a truth mean you are sure of deserving it? Where could we find such certainty? Ah, to grow into what we try to observe."[10] The endeavor to find truth never remains a theoretical effort. If it does, it loses its sincerity and noble beauty. The effort is personal, the struggle of the self for authenticity. Truth yields its traces in the authenticity of the self. The authentic self struggles for truth. It is alive because this struggle has become its substance. But there is another endeavor which comes forth in the persistent question: Am I worthy of this truth? We are never worthy of the truth. We are worthy only of its hints, its traces, its sounds, and its images. With these we find the meaning of authenticity, which we are always finding, attempting to become one with it. For the Jew, there can be no separation between the goodness of life and the need to search for the truth of God. To the world, the Jew cried out: God is truth. There is only the unique oneness of God, the truth of truths. This he proclaimed to those for whom the gods represented many truths, who believed that nature was truth, that its laws of necessity were truths, and that the reasonable doubts of men, their sophistic argumentations, embodied truths which man could not surpass. The Jew knew that truth was embodied in a book and that it was this book which kept the people from the labyrinth of self–indulgence and unmitigated skepticism. The book embodied the negation of self–deification, the negation of nature; it embodied the freedom of man which was persistently identified with the receptivity of seeing and hearing, with the presence of the absent word and the uncontrollable power of the image.

"What we do deserve – our share of the book – " Jabès stated, "lies hidden perhaps between the lines of the book. No doubt, the strength of creation depends upon not knowing this."[11] Hidden are the mysteries of the book, hidden in the depths of the words lie the divine signs which were left in the creation as God withdrew from it and left it to the laws of necessity. The divine signs are concealed. Their revelation would bring forth the end of creation. They are veils which hover over creation, allowing it to become the work of man, the realm in which man finds the

---

[10]Ibid.
[11]Ibid.

concealments of nature which he struggles to conquer. There are limits to man's knowledge and imagination. Without these limits, man could no longer understand the natural and human world. He would convert it inordinately, manipulate it destructively, and reform it arbitrarily. Man's pretense to divinity is demonic, but within the human circumference man challenges these demonic intentions and preserves the rational course of human development. Man must be preserved from the highest degrees of knowledge which destroy his capacity to control their implementation. Nothing is more dangerous to man than the knowledge which surpasses his moral capacity to give it form and beauty. The book remains concealed. It reveals man's incapacity to comprehend it. The book can be spoken of, but never is the reality of the book, and words which speak of it, identifiable.

Jabès remarked that "we can never know the value of the book. It can only be measured in terms of its resistance against the abyss. And who knows to what point the book can be lost?"[12] The book is present only in the reality of its absence. Its presence indicates the signs, the traces, and the concealed sounds which flow from it. The book is everywhere. It is like the sands of the desert, fleeting and revealing, moving, and changing forms. For men the book is in exile, a nomadic text which is always above and beyond the text of what we call a book. The book is present, but only as a book that is lost, unknown, and invisible. The mystery of the book is the constancy of its presence to the imagination, the source of our images and metaphors. We are embraced by, and in, the book, and yet the book is absent. We are embraced by a book which allows man to think of the embracing book. The power of the book lies in the possibilities it gives to man, making it possible for him to penetrate the mystery of the I think. The book is the light but it is more; it relates to the exile of a people, and, in this way, to all humankind. The book is the light which has become a social history, whose landmarks are the desert, the exile, and the absence of the divine which in absence becomes the guiding force in the odyssey of the book. The book wanders like those who live from its concealment. Like the animals, man dwells in dwellings; unlike them, he seeks to escape from them. His life begins in his departure. His loyalties are seemingly to families and nations, but in the midst of these loyalties are the calls of the spirit, causing him to look upward and observe the powers which lie above his existence. In this uplifting of the spirit, man finds another dimension of life. This dimension is life and more than life. It is paradoxical and parabolic. The words which describe it are contradictory. They reveal an interplay of paradoxical forces attempting to link the book with man. But these links

---

[12]Ibid.

are meaningful when man discovers that they can be formed only through the exile of the spirit wandering the sands and the seas.

The poet said that "the Jew inherited the Name and, at the same time, lost his place on earth. The nomad takes on himself the unstated Name."[13] There is loneliness in the Name, a loneliness which comes from the loss of dwelling among the peoples of the world. But there is another loneliness, a metaphysical loneliness which has its origin in the Name, in the hearing of the Name which pierces the din of daily life. This is the hearing of the Name which is veiled in concealment. Metaphysical loneliness allows us to hear the din of mankind and be silent in it, to be a part of it and yet beyond it. Loneliness belongs to the exile, to the wanderer of the desert. We dwell in a place, and we are exiled from a place. Loneliness begins when we are called from our dwelling and can only say, away from here. Our departure is our reality; the walls must fall and we must journey, guided only by the concealment of the Name. The Jew is the spiritual nomad. In his nomadic journeys he touches the permanencies of the world, the habits and customs of people. He joins them and becomes absorbed in them, but he is quickly reminded that he is only a nomad and must go on, to other lands and realms. Never can he dwell in one land with its tradition. He is the eternal stranger reminded again and again of his exile. He is permitted to enter a land but not to remain. The book is silent and there is only a silent presence. The exile is silent and from this silence comes the blood of persecution, of those who fear the strangers of exile, fear their book which they cannot touch nor hear. This book defies their definitions and their traditions, their temples and worship. This is the book of the nomad.

"The act of writing may be nothing but an act of controlled violence, the time it takes to move on to a new stage of violence. The book explodes with infuriating legibility. All shattered writing has the form of a key."[14] The poet has grasped the word as a shattering experience. He has revealed himself in the word. He has created with the word, turning from the reality about him to realities which he knew had not been touched, heard, or seen. Reality yielded reality as words exploded into words. Each step of the journey was a preparation for another experience, a "key" to a new realm of being, a new possibility of the powers of nonbeing, of negation and absence. The poet seeks to be free, to shatter the relationships which ordinarily confined and explained his world, which were the creations of science and the precision of measurement and repetition. The poet knows the creative power of the word, the violence which it embodies and the images it creates. Man is

---

[13]Ibid.
[14]Ibid., 10.

the consequence of his use of the word. He paints and sculptures with the word. He creates his being with it. The word is the violence which tears one generation from the other, which links one to the other. In the contradictions, the word discovers the violence which is the creation of thought, which is the poetic muse. Jabès spoke of the act of writing as "controlled violence." With these two words he opened the world to powers that lay within the human experience, that revealed its divinely crushing moments. Not in the quietude of an image do we discover God, but in violence, in the shattering reality of man's capacity to name and rename things. In this controlled violence man finds a hint of divinity.

Literature is the violence of the word. The writer doesn't fully control the words which emerge from the pen. They grow from each other. "One letter in common is enough for two words to know each other." The writer doesn't create, but discovers that he is being created, moved by the relationships of phrases, ideas, and forms. The I launches forth with Napoleonic powers, and believes that there are worlds to be conquered. The violence of the endeavor is invigorating and revelatory, but this violence is confronted by another which lies in the words themselves. The violence in the words forces us to realize that what has been forged and molded is not a life brought forth from the dead, but the emergence of a life that yearns to see the light, that is life before man understood it to be life. Man is always awakening to life. He does not create it. He seeks to find ways to bring forth the light which dwells in the created forms he opens himself. "Light also is a word which begets other, explosive words."[15] The poet is sensitive to experiences which few other men share. He knows that "all other life ceases in the life put into words." He knows that the word hides and reveals. It imprisons and liberates, but the word is always becoming the word, always emerging from itself, calling forth itself and others. The I which moves to conquer the world of forms finds its limits within itself. Wanting to reform the world in its image, it discovers the world already formed, waiting to be confronted. In this confrontation, literature is nurtured and developed. What is given cannot merely be seen or heard, mirrored or shown. It must be transformed and transfigured. The process, if there is such, is filled with the unexpected, the unknown, and the unconditioned. Authenticity of method depends upon the free powers of the imagination limited only by the powers of reason.

"O crumbled word. O book turned to dust. You thought," remarked Jabès, "you had done with letters, with symbols. But is that possible? Dust begets more dust."[16] The book created becomes a book of dust. We

---

[15]Ibid., 11.
[16]Ibid., 11.

faced the disappearance of the book as we have faced the disappearance of art and science. Disappearance belongs to our finiteness, to the death which is identified with it. But we create in spite of death which hovers over all which we do. Death forces us to yield to despair or to fortitude. Death lives in the reality which we bring forth, as it lives in those of us who create in hope of remembrance. We want to be remembered. We have few reasons to explain the crumbling book, the forgotten art of commentary and love. We have no explanation to account for the selectivity of the generations. We know only the violence in us which forces us to write, knowing the dust which will gather about our books. We write in defiance. We are conscious of the fickleness of the generations, but our need is vital, our love brave, and our dreams uncontrollable. Jabès led us through the valleys of contradictions, between the mountains of tears. There is no promised land; there is only the image. There are only vague hopes and visions, and, above all, love of the invisible. Never can we put aside the night, the unconquerable darkness which defies every flicker of light. We walk in this darkness into a darkness terrorized by the light it seeks to extinguish. It is the darkness which wants to rule alone, to return man to the cave, to suppress his word and dominate his activity. Darkness is the power which excites our violence, but crushes its creative forces. If it could suppress our violence, it would suppress our divinity. The world would remain darkness with particles of crushed light.

"O spent point, infinite defense of the book. A single grain of sand holds out against the desert."[17] These last words sound throughout our being. In this "single grain" lives the violence of defiance, the unconquerable point which doesn't disappear nor fade away. This last grain is man's nobility, the point which cannot be tamed nor brought into conformity with circumstances. This "single grain of sand" is a spark of the divine fire left in man, separating him from other beings, making him unique in the universe. With this "single grain of sand" the poet writes his odyssey, the painter creates his visions, the scientist formulates his conceptualizations. Man refuses to settle into a dwelling, fixing his images and determining his place in nature. The sand is an irritant, making man uncomfortable and dissatisfied. It sends him forth to find new lands, new wonders and dreams. From one dwelling to another, man travels both the physical and spiritual worlds. His wandering makes him the exile wherever he finds rest. His eyes see beyond what he perceives, his ears listen to what is beyond what he hears. There is that need to seek new dimensions of being, to transcend the given, to force the phenomenon to yield new directions and forms. In

---

[17]Ibid.

piercing the given, causing it to yield the secrets of its being, man re-creates the world with reason and imagination. Nothing remains defined and engraven. Every perspective, attitude, concept is expanded and surpassed. Every vision forges a new and different insight. Life and death move outward and away from each other. Their companionship is firm and intimate. Man listens to the sounds of the universe, and his thoughts take him to unseen lands, where he wanders like the nomad, conscious not only of what is below or before him, but what is above him. Like the moving dunes, all is changing. With this vision, the poet breaks through the fortresses of habit and tradition. With the violence of dissatisfaction he seeks to shatter every graven image and word. He seeks to show how dependent the creation is upon this dissatisfaction, how deeply its forms and mysteries await the force of the metaphor and metonymy.

Conclusion

We gather together the words of the poet. We hear their names: the book, the desert, the exile, the nomad, the Jew, the violence of the imagination. With these words come other names, like Sarah, Yukel, Yaël, Elya, Aely, and El. We pronounce these words. We hear sounds, but these are not enough to create their reality. They cause us to remember relationships and events, but these are vague. We have to imagine the stories; some we know already. The poet asked us to write with him. He left us the whiteness of large margins. He called forth to our imagination. He asked for our companionship. He gave us his voice and his word. The poet wrote commentaries which are endless impossibilities. He made us wonder about the meaning of the presence of God's absence. He brought us into the world of the metaphor, the metonymy, the analogy. He challenged us with an odyssey of thinking and imagining. The wandering of the Jew fascinated him. The book always accompanied the poet, the exiled Jew. It led him to explore the commentaries which were created about it. Aphorisms took the place of narratives. Thoughts clustered about thoughts as images emerged from images. I explored with Jabès this realm of the desert, the shifting sands. I listened to their voices, to their echoes. I was drawn closer and closer to the sounds of the poet. These were the songs of the moving dunes, of the stars in the darkness of the heavens. I journeyed with him, facing the unknown and the unexpected. I searched with him for the authenticity of being. I found more exploration, more wondrous adventures.

Our concluding words come from a place on a path, a resting place. In a short time, we will begin again the journey. The poet holds out his hand to us. He wants us to follow him. There is so much more to be seen and heard. The journey has just begun. A long, long time ago, the poet sang to us. Once we heard the sounds, they never left us. We refuse to let them go. We repeat them to ourselves again and again. Death quiets the poet. We weep at the approach of death. The poet will be silent in us. This is our death.

Afterword

I knew that after years of reading Jabès's poetry his thought would change into many sounds and forms. I was reading a poet who was forever becoming a poet, a philosopher who was continuously changing into a philosopher. This was peculiarly alien to my thinking. Suddenly, I discovered that it was not. I had become extremely close to what I liked to call nomadic thinking. Jabès showed me how the poet creates his forms in multiple conversations and commentaries. No, he did not give lessons. He was responding to a book which couldn't be written, defined, or limited. He responded to the unknown, the undefinable. It was the unknown which was both reality and beyond reality. It was always with us, and yet transcended whatever we thought. It was absence in presence. It was a futile yearning to comprehend the incomprehensible, to approach the unapproachable. Wherever I turned, I was in the presence of the book. When I yearned to reach out to it, it faded from my sight. In this word *absence* lay the secret of mortal thinking. It informed me that what I wanted to grasp, I could not have, what I wanted to make my reality, would never be mine. Being and having were abysmally separated from each other. Never would they be identified with each other. I lay in the abyss. Thoughts clustered about me, but when I wanted to give them form, they fled in all directions. They gyrated about me. I knew that the gyration was feeble and they would scatter and leave me in chaos. The dunes of sand were never the same. My imagination grew tired. I could only sleep and await the morning. I wanted to begin again to think of the book and the wondering which is in the conversation and the commentary to the book.

I remembered the text in the last of the seven volumes of *The Book of Questions*. Often, I do not remember the text and I reread it. I feel as if I have read an unknown text. Remembering plays nomadic tunes. I enjoy listening to them but I often grow weary. I feel as if I can't escape *The Book of Questions*, which had made me a child in my devotion to it. I know that this is true and untrue. I am with the book and distant from it.

Its absence fills my presence and its presence forces me to be conscious of its absence. I know that what is fully present is idolatry. I know that the book is there and everywhere, but never here. It can't be here.

I recalled a text in *El, or The Last Book.* It read:

> I must warn you: writing leads to suicide. Is it only one human life that is at stake in the act of writing? And what is a human life compared to the life of a word? Perhaps, nothing. Or all. Or all of a Nothing or again Nothing of an All.

> Thus they died. Thus he again picked up his pen, and this natural, almost automatic gesture, suddenly seemed to be so loaded with unknown forces that he shivered. (77)

Yes, writing bears its fate, and like the scorpion, it injects its infection into every being it encounters. Often the wound is overcome, but the mark of its infection is never erased. We are the children of the wound. We are the tribe of those who are marked.

This mark is there for everyone to see and hear. It creates its own music. We are the children of the word. Our death is precious to our enemies. The word is always with us. It is the call which identifies us. With it we are recognized by all men who know the dangers which we exude. The word is terrifying. There is no way to hide from it. It must be crushed. We must be killed or else the word will be corrupted by those in whom we find refuge.

I have traveled metaphorically with Jabès for many years. I have not followed him. He can't be followed. In journeying with him, I traveled alone. Loneliness is the way of the imagination. The word can't be shared. There are resemblances, but even these do not erase the loneliness. The word is never my companion. It is fickle and finds many listeners. It can't be mine, and yet I yearn for it to be mine. I yearn to bring it into my dwelling, but it will not dwell with me. It goes its own way. This I have learned. I am still learning what I have learned. The echoes do not cease. I have taken Reb Prato's words: "Do not neglect the echo. You live by echoes."[1] His words teach me that there are only echoes. These are rarely clear, but we struggle to hear them. We will never hear them. We pretend. This is all we can do. Never will our hearing be adequate to the word. Never will the word find a place in our being. The word is a nomad. It wanders. We yearn for the nomadic word. The word smiles at our yearning. It can do nothing else.

I move in many directions. I live in fear of vertigo and madness. Nothing saves me from them. I know that death silences them, but death is the most terrifying of all destinies. I shrink from it. These are the

---

[1] *The Book of Questions*, 1:39.

endless circular movements. I move within the endless cycles of commentaries and I tremble. I fear my trembling. This is the fate of the nomadic wanderer.